THE 50 GREATEST DESIGNERS

THE 50 GREATEST DESIGNERS

THE PEOPLE WHO HAVE CREATED OUR ENVIRONMENT

TOM MAY

SIRIUS

This edition published in 2025 by Sirius Publishing, a division of
Arcturus Publishing Limited,
26/27 Bickels Yard, 151–153 Bermondsey Street,
London SE1 3HA

Copyright © Arcturus Holdings Limited

All rights reserved. No part of this publication may be reproduced, stored
in a retrieval system, or transmitted, in any form or by any means,
electronic, mechanical, photocopying, recording or otherwise, without
prior written permission in accordance with the provisions of the
Copyright Act 1956 (as amended). Any person or persons who do any
unauthorised act in relation to this publication may be liable to criminal
prosecution and civil claims for damages.

ISBN: 978-1-3988-4259-5
AD010970UK

Printed in Malaysia

Contents

Introduction 6
William Morris (1834–1896). 8
Ferdinand Porsche (1875–1951) 12
Eileen Gray (1878–1976) 16
Harley Earl (1893–1969). 20
Poul Henningsen (1894–1967) 24
Harry Beck (1902–1974). 28
Marcel Breuer (1902–1981) 32
Elizabeth Friedländer (1903–1984) 36
Jacqueline Groag (1903–1986) 40
Charlotte Perriand (1903–1999) 44
Eva Zeisel (1906–2011). 48
Charles and Ray Eames
(1907–1978 / 1912–1988). 52
Marianne Straub (1909–1994) 56
Paul Rand (1914–1996). 60
Florence Knoll (1917–2019) 64
Lucienne Day (1917–2010). 68
Saul Bass (1920–1966) 72
Milton Glaser (1920–2020) 76
Jacqueline Casey (1927–1992) 80
Maija Isola (1927–2001) 84
Adrian Frutiger (1928–2015) 88
Kenji Ekuan (1929–2015) 92
Massimo Vignelli (1931–2014). 96
Terence Conran (1931–2020) 100
Dieter Rams (B.1932) 104

Margaret Calvert (B.1936) 108
Rosmarie Tissi (B.1937). 112
Giorgetto Giugiaro (B.1937) 116
James Dyson (B.1947). 120
Erik Spiekermann (B.1947) 124
Paula Scher (B.1948) 128
Lonnie Johnson (B.1949) 132
Philippe Starck (B.1949) 136
Paola Navone (B.1950). 140
Ahn Sang-soo (B.1952) 144
Susan Kare (B.1954) 148
Art Sims (B.1954) 152
Naoto Fukasawa (B.1956) 156
Carol Twombly (B.1959). 160
Karim Rashid (B.1960) 164
Stefan Sagmeister (B.1962) 168
Gail Anderson (B.1962) 172
Hella Jongerius (B.1963). 176
Marc Newson (B.1963) 180
Jonathan Ive (B.1967) 184
Kenneth Cobonpue (B.1968). 188
Es Devlin (B.1971) 192
Cas Holman (B.1974) 196
Pum Lefebure (B.1974). 200
Naihan Li (B.1981). 204

Picture credits/Acknowledgements . . 208

Above: The Conran Shop

INTRODUCTION

Design is a discipline that's often perceived as rarefied and inward looking. But in fact the opposite is true. The work of designers impacts our lives on a day-to-day, if not minute-by-minute, basis. And yet we rarely notice, because the ultimate aim of design is to be invisible.

We all know when a thing or service is badly designed because it looks ugly, is difficult to use, or simply doesn't work properly. Otherwise, though, we rarely register the design work that's gone into it. And this helps to explain why even the greatest designers are invisible to most people outside of the profession.

Ask the average person to name five famous actors, writers, or musicians and few will struggle. Ask for five famous designers and the response will likely be very different. Yet despite working in relative obscurity, designers have created the very fabric of the world around us.

They are the alchemists of the everyday, the conjurers of function and desire. From the heights of haute couture to the gritty realms of industrial design, the best designers' fingerprints touch every surface of our lives. Their creations whisper in the curves of furniture, sing in the cadence of a well-placed typeface, roar in the sleek lines of a machine.

INTRODUCTION

This book is an ode to 50 such luminaries, a chronicle of inspired brilliance woven with threads of innovation, audacity, and unwavering passion. Within these pages you'll encounter incredible minds who have fought against convention, built empires from scraps, and dared to redefine the very nature of what design could be.

Each designer in this book is a universe unto themselves, a complex tapestry woven with threads of talent, perseverance, and a touch of serendipity. And each chapter will trace how their most iconic and influential design work emerged from a complex interplay of personal circumstances and the grand sweep of history.

But this book is not just about individuals. It's also about the grand, ever-evolving narrative of design itself. Each of these 50 personal stories is an opportunity to explore how design reflects and shapes our culture, both fuelling revolutions and offering comfort in times of strife. And ultimately this helps us respond to one of the biggest questions of our time: In a world saturated with stuff, yet struggling with the need for sustainability, what role should design play?

Above: Mac Cube computer

WILLIAM MORRIS

THIS DESIGNER'S NAME IS OFTEN INVOKED WHEN PEOPLE WISH TO INVITE BEAUTY INTO THEIR HOMES.

BRITISH
1834–1896

HIGHLIGHTS
Wallpaper, fabrics, furniture, stained glass, books

CHARACTERISTICS
Handcrafting, traditional techniques, natural motifs, geometric shapes and patterns

Opposite: One of Morris's most famous patterns – Strawberry Thief (1883)

William Morris's name is known by millions of people, primarily due to his timeless wallpaper designs. Never out of production since their launch in 1864, these intricate creations, characterized by nature-inspired motifs and rich colours, remain as popular in the 21st century as they were in the 19th and 20th. But this is just the tip of the iceberg of what William Morris gave to the world. His legacy is less about specific designs and more about the way he shaped our understanding of what design should be, at a time when society had been turned upside down by the Industrial Revolution of 1760–1840.

Morris was born in Walthamstow, Essex (now London) in 1834 to a wealthy middle-class family. He enjoyed a happy, privileged childhood, but his father died when he was 14 and he was sent to Marlborough College in Wiltshire, where he suffered three years of bullying and homesickness. In 1852 he went to study classics at Oxford University, where he became strongly inspired by the art and culture of the medieval period. After graduating, he became a leading member of the Arts and Crafts movement, which campaigned against the deterioration in standards resulting from mechanization.

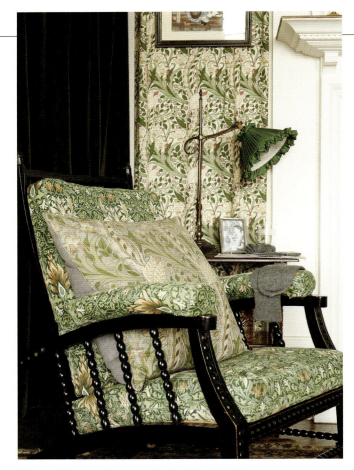

Above: The morning room chair at Standen House

Today none of this would be hugely controversial, but at the time it went very much against the grain. Morris wrote, "There is no square mile of earth's inhabitable surface that is not beautiful in its own way, if we men will only abstain from wilfully destroying that beauty." Eschewing mass production, he taught himself tapestry weaving and re-established hand-blocked printing for cotton and linen fabrics. His designs were known for their use of natural forms and motifs, such as leaves, flowers, and animals, and he also favoured simple geometric shapes and patterns.

While his upbringing might have pointed him towards elitism, Morris was a strong advocate for art education, and believed everyone should have access to high-quality design and craftsmanship. As part of a book-design renaissance inspired by the Arts and Crafts movement, he founded Kelmscott Press in 1891. The company produced limited editions of illuminated-style print books that were renowned for their elegant design and typography.

Morris believed that factory production had led to a decline in the quality of design and craftsmanship, and wanted to see a return to traditional methods—not just for their own sake, but so that people could have beautiful and functional objects that would improve their lives. And he wasn't just an academic theorist, but put his principles into practice. In 1861, he co-founded the firm Morris, Marshall, Faulkner & Co., whose "decorative arts" (what we would now call interior design) products—including tapestries, wallpaper, fabrics, furniture, and stained-glass windows—became highly fashionable and influential throughout the Victorian period.

Morris's approach placed a strong emphasis on craftsmanship and the use of high-quality materials, and championed traditional techniques such as hand-weaving, dyeing, and printing. He clearly held this belief from a young age. On a family trip to London in 1851, when he was just 16, he refused to enter the Great Exhibition—which championed the products of the Victorian age—because of his objections to machine production.

This publishing string to Morris's bow is often downplayed, but it was hugely influential—partly because his layout designs effortlessly fused decoration and readability, and partly because he inspired generations of graphic designers to found small print-publishing houses of their own.

More generally, because Morris favoured the natural and handcrafted over mass manufacturing, he has occasionally been described as the "original hipster." (The fact that he had a beard and lived in Walthamstow adds to this conceit.) But while members of that modern tribe pride themselves on achieving work-life balance, Morris was relentless in his work ethic.

Along with running his businesses, he was a writer and poet who wrote 23 books. Most notably, they include *The Defence of Guenevere and Other Poems*, and *The Earthly Paradise*, a collection of poems inspired by Norse mythology and medieval legends. These works played a big part in establishing the modern fantasy genre that dominates popular culture, as seen in TV shows such as *Game of Thrones*. Clearly, multitasking felt natural to him; he wrote, "If a chap can't compose an epic poem while he's weaving tapestry, he had better shut up, he'll never do any good at all."

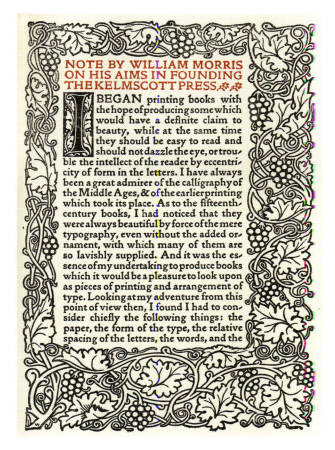

Above: A note written and printed by William Morris on his aims in founding Kelmscott Press

Morris was politically and socially active too; he was a member of the Socialist League and was involved in various campaigns for workers' rights and social justice. He worked tirelessly for the cause, often meeting his comrades several times a week and giving hundreds of lectures; he was arrested in 1885 for disorderly conduct at a trial of left-wing protesters. And he didn't only object to the accumulation of wealth on personal grounds. As he wrote, "The greatest foe to art is luxury, art cannot live in its atmosphere." Similarly, he said, "I don't want art for a few, any more than education for a few, or freedom for a few."

All aspects of his fascinating and inspirational life are celebrated at the William Morris Gallery in Walthamstow, a museum set in a Grade II-listed Georgian home within Lloyd Park. Admission is free, in keeping with Morris's values of making great art and design accessible to all.

Left: Standen House in East Grinstead, England, is famed for its William Morris interiors

Right: The iconic Porsche 550 Spyder

FERDINAND PORSCHE

FERDINAND PORSCHE IS FAMED FOR THE COMPANY AND VEHICLES THAT BEAR HIS NAME. BUT HIS LEGACY EXTENDS BEYOND THESE LIMITS AND CONTINUES TO INFLUENCE AUTOMOTIVE DESIGN, OVER A CENTURY ON.

GERMAN-AUSTRIAN
1875–1951

HIGHLIGHTS
Volkswagen Beetle, Porsche 356, Porsche 550 Spyder, Mercedes-Benz SSK

CHARACTERISTICS
Lightweight construction, functionality and simplicity, rear-engine layout, innovative technologies

Born in 1875 in the town of Maffersdorf, Austria-Hungary (now Vratislavice nad Nisou, Czech Republic), Porsche was exposed to engineering and mechanics from an early age, as his father was a master panel-beater. By the age of 14 he was conducting experiments with electricity in a workshop he'd set up at home; due to his father's disapproval, the experiments were a secret.

At 18, after completing both his plumber apprenticeship and the state trade school in Reichenberg, he got his first apprenticeship, at Béla Egger & Co. Electrical Company (now ABB) in Vienna. He quickly rose through the ranks. Then, in 1898, Porsche developed the world's first electric car, the Egger-Lohner electric vehicle C2 Phaeton, also known as the P1.

That simple fact bears repeating. Despite what current discourse may suggest, the e-vehicle is by no means a modern invention, but dates back to the century before last. In fact, Porsche could be described as the godfather of environmentally sustainable motoring, because two years later he also designed the world's first hybrid car, the Semper Vivus.

Above: Porsche designed several cars for Mercedes in the 1920s, including the Mercedes Benz-SSK

Back at the start of the 20th century, however, these innovations were more of a curiosity than anything else. The world had a seemingly unending supply of oil, nobody knew about global warming, and even automotive pollution wasn't much of an issue because of the scarcity of cars. But what these designs did highlight was Porsche's vision and genius—and there was more to come.

Between 1923 and 1929, he worked on the design of a number of Mercedes cars, including the two-litre Mercedes Kompressor, the Mercedes Benz Type 630, and the Mercedes Benz-SSK.

> *"IN THE BEGINNING I LOOKED AROUND AND, NOT FINDING THE AUTOMOBILE OF MY DREAMS, DECIDED TO BUILD IT MYSELF…"*
>
> FERDINAND PORSCHE

Below: One of Porsche's most popular designs, the shapely VW Beetle

Opposite: Porsche's love of beautiful curves is also apparent in the 1963 Porsche 356 C

Then, in 1931, he founded Porsche AG, a sports-car manufacturer, which carved out a reputation for high-performance vehicles that were both elegant and efficient. And Porsche didn't just help design them; he also raced them and had quite an accomplished career behind the wheel.

Perhaps his most famous creation was the Volkswagen Type 1, commonly known as the Beetle, which was commissioned in 1934 by Adolf Hitler. The Nazi dictator wanted to create a car that was affordable and could be driven on the newly constructed autobahns. The vehicle's name is German for "people's car," and Porsche designed it to be simple, reliable, and easy to manufacture, with a streamlined body and an air-cooled engine mounted in the rear.

Before that time, most cars had their engines mounted in the front, which made them heavy and difficult to manoeuvre. Porsche's genius was to realize that by placing the engine in the rear, he could improve the car's handling and stability. The Beetle eventually became one of the best-selling cars of all time, with 23 million units sold during its 81-year run.

Unlike the big, flashy cars of the era—which were characterized by chrome, fins, and grandiosity—the VW Beetle's small size and teardrop shape gave it real personality, and it was much loved by generations of young people. It even became a star of Disney movies as Herbie, a magical car with a mind of its own; more recently it became the "base mode" of the Transformers character Bumblebee in the eponymous 2018 movie.

During the Second World War, Porsche's company shifted to the production of military vehicles for the army, including the Tiger tank and the Ferdinand tank destroyer. Following Germany's defeat, Porsche was jailed by the French for 22 months on charges of war crimes; he was eventually released due to lack of evidence.

In 1948, Porsche introduced the firm's first production sports car, the 356, which had a lightweight body, rear-wheel drive, and sleek look. In the 1950s came the 550 Spyder, a lightweight racing car powered by a flat-four engine, which featured a distinctive "gull-wing" door design.

FERDINAND PORSCHE

Many of Porsche's innovations and ideas were adopted by other companies. For example, the rear-mounted engine and independent suspension system in the Beetle inspired the design of the Fiat 500 and the Renault Dauphine, while the use of a lightweight, tubular steel frame in the 550 Spyder was adopted by other race-car manufacturers.

Automotive design is ultimately a collaborative effort; no one person ever creates a car from start to finish by themselves. But Porsche certainly believed in leading from the front. "Committees are, by nature, timid," he said. "They are based on the premise of safety in numbers; content to survive inconspicuously, rather than take risks and move independently ahead. Without independence, without the freedom for new ideas to be tried, to fail, and to ultimately succeed, the world will not move ahead, but rather live in fear of its own potential."

He died in 1951 at the age of 76, leaving behind a legacy of design innovation. This was partly continued by his son, Ferry Porsche, and his grandson Ferdinand Alexander Porsche, who died in 2012, ending an astonishing dynasty.

The cars of the elder Ferdinand Porsche are remembered for their simplicity, reliability, and functionality as well as being style icons of their era. You can see some of his most important work at the Porsche Museum in Zuffenhausen, a suburb of Stuttgart. Porsche himself had a neat way of summarizing his career. "In the beginning I looked around and, not finding the automobile of my dreams, decided to build it myself," he said.

EILEEN GRAY

HER ICONIC FURNITURE DESIGNS BLENDED TRADITIONAL CRAFTSMANSHIP WITH MODERNIST PRINCIPLES.

IRISH
1878–1976

HIGHLIGHTS
Bibendum Chair, Transat Chair, Dragons Armchair, Non Conformist Chair

CHARACTERISTICS
Sleek and minimalist, comfortable and functional, playful and timeless

Opposite: Gray's folding screen done in her characteristic lacquer finish

Irish-born furniture designer and architect Eileen Gray received proper recognition in her lifetime, but only by a whisker. She finally received the acclaim she deserved at the age of 94, just four years before her death.

She was born into an aristocratic Irish family in Enniscorthy in 1878, and her father, James McLaren Smith, was a landscape painter. In 1898 she went to study drawing and painting at the Slade School of Fine Art in London. However, she soon shifted her focus to Japanese and East Asian lacquerware: objects, tableware, furniture, and other items decoratively covered with lacquer.

She studied the practice with experts and was so dedicated that she even developed lacquer disease, a painful form of contact dermatitis. Nonetheless, Gray managed to develop her own distinct style by combining two Japanese techniques: red Negoro lacquer (a minimalist style featuring a patina of red and black lacquer layers) and *maki-e* (which involves drawing pictures, patterns, and letters with lacquer then dusting it with gold or silver powder).

This work brought her to the attention of the French avant-garde, and she was soon being commissioned by the wealthy citizens of Paris to produce lacquered screens, panels, and furniture for their homes. Gray's work was characterized by refined forms, bold colours, and intricate surface patterns.

In 1922 she set up her own gallery in Paris. At the time, a female store owner was highly unusual, which is perhaps why she gave it a man's name—Galerie Jean Désert—and why her business cards ambiguously read "Jean Désert et E: Gray."

During the 1920s and 1930s she became a leading exponent of Modernism, a movement associated with innovation in materials, minimalism in product design, and a focus on abstraction. Gray worked closely with many of its best-known figures, including Swiss-French architect and designer Le Corbusier and Dutch architect J.J.P. Oud. Gray's own use of chrome, steel tube, and glass furniture as early as 1925 was strikingly ahead of its time, and still appears modern and stylish.

One of Gray's best-known works, the Bibendum chair, was designed in 1926. Taking its name from a resemblance to the Michelin Man, it's made of curved, upholstered tubes. In 1927 came the Transat chair, a lightweight folding chair inspired by the deck chairs used on ocean liners. Made of beechwood and canvas, it is notable for its simple elegance. Also designed in 1926, Gray's Non Conformist chair was made of chrome-plated tubular steel; it featured a simple geometric design and had a padded leather seat and backrest. Its clean lines and minimalist design made it an enduring favourite among fans of Modernist furniture.

Gray's attention eventually drifted away from furniture and towards architecture, which she became proficient in despite having no formal training in the discipline. Today her work in this area is celebrated most for E-1027. Designed in partnership with her lover, Romanian-born architecture critic Jean Badovici, this holiday home overlooking Roquebrune-Cap-Martin in the south of France was

"THE FUTURE PROJECTS LIGHT, THE PAST ONLY CLOUDS."
Eileen Gray

Left: The Transat Chair designed in 1927

EILEEN GRAY

Left: The Dragons armchair from the Yves Saint Laurent and Pierre Berge' Collection at Christie's London

formulated on Le Corbusier's manifesto *Five Points of Modern Architecture*, namely pilotis (pillars), roof garden, open floor plan, long horizontal window, and open facades (As for the house's name, the E stood for Eileen; the 10 for Jean, J being the 10th letter in the alphabet; the 2 for Badovici; and the 7 for Gray.)

In general, though, Gray fell short of getting the respect and acclaim she deserved during her lifetime. However, she remained endlessly optimistic and forward-looking, stating, "The future projects light, the past only clouds." It was only in 1972, when she was 94, that art historian Joseph Rykwert brought her to prominence after publishing a celebratory essay in the journal Architectural Review.

Since Gray's death in 1976, her work has been exhibited in Ireland, Paris, and New York, and some of her pieces have changed hands for millions. In 2009, for example, her Dragons armchair, created in 1917, went for €21,905,000 at Christie's, setting a record for a single piece of decorative art.

Gray's architecture, too, has been reappraised, not to mention reconstructed. This was necessary because the E-1027 home fell victim to a number of disasters. First, Le Corbusier vandalized it by encouraging Badovici to place huge murals on its walls. Whether this was done out of admiration or spite, it was hugely disrespectful given Gray's belief that interior design and architecture needed to be unified and harmonious. But worse was to come.

During the war, the building was occupied by Italian, then German, soldiers, who used it for target practice. The house later changed hands, and by the 1980s it was rumoured to have become a drug and orgy den. In 1996 the owner was murdered, and after that the house rapidly deteriorated. But it has since been restored, and was opened to the public in 2021.

Gray continued to innovate into old age. In the 1970s she began experimenting with celluloid, and just before her death she was working on a shocking-pink screen that anticipated the aesthetics of the punk era. But while she never settled on a single discipline or artistic approach, her entire body of work was unified by a single principle, which she summarized thus: "A house is not a machine to live in. It is the shell of man, his extension, his release, his spiritual emanation."

Eileen Gray died in 1976, aged 98. She is buried in Père-Lachaise cemetery in Paris, but her grave is not identifiable because her family failed to pay the licence fee. Anyone wishing to learn more about her work and fascinating life should watch Gray Matters, a 2014 documentary written and directed by Marco Orsini. The National Museum of Ireland also hosts a permanent exhibition of her work, which features such items as the E1027 Adjustable Table and the Non Conformist chair along with family photos, lacquering tools, and personal ephemera.

Above: Eileen Gray exhibition, National Museum of Ireland

HARLEY EARL

"A GREYHOUND IS MORE ATTRACTIVE THAN A BULLDOG."

Harley Earl

Harley Earl changed the way cars were designed in a fundamental way. Before he went to work at General Motors, most cars essentially looked the same. If a buyer wanted theirs to stand out, they'd buy the basic version from the manufacturer, then send it to a coach builder to get it customized.

One such coach builder was J.W. Earl of Hollywood, California, whose son Harley was born in 1893. Following school, he studied at Stanford but dropped out to join the family firm.

By the time Harley was 25, he'd become lead designer. At that point he was headhunted by GM to work on Cadillac's more affordable car line, LaSalle. His job title was "design consultant" – the first of his kind in the industry.

The LaSalle was a huge hit, and it led GM to launch the industry's first formalized styling department in 1928. It was known as the Art and Color Section, and later the Styling Section. Earl remained head of design there until 1958.

He wasn't just a pioneer, either, but would introduce a string of innovations that would change car design forever. Most significantly, he was one of the first people to make extensive use of clay modelling in the design process. This involved creating physical models of cars that could be evaluated and refined before production. Even in today's digital age, clay modelling plays a vital role in automotive development.

HARLEY EARL

AMERICAN
1893–1969

HIGHLIGHTS
Chevrolet Nomad, Cadillac Eldorado Brougham, early-1950s Buicks, Chevrolet Corvette

CHARACTERISTICS
Bold styling, streamlined and aerodynamic, "low and long," tailfins, wraparound windshields

Below: Harley Earl (in the car) and Larry Peter Fisher with the LaSalle, 1927

Above: A model poses with the Buick Wildcat II concept car designed by Harley Earl in 1954

In 1939, Earl styled and built the Buick Y-Job, the motor industry's first concept car or "dream car." While one-off custom cars had been made before, this was the first built by a mass manufacturer for the sole purpose of eliciting public reaction to new design ideas. And the firsts continued: For the 1948 Oldsmobile, Earl was involved in the development of the first fully automatic transmission. This made it easier for drivers to shift gears, and improved the overall driving experience.

For the 1948 Cadillac, he introduced the first automotive tailfin, a motif inspired by the twin-boom tail of the Lockheed P-38 Lightning aircraft. Earl is also celebrated for his love of chrome trim and for the introduction of the wraparound windshield, which gave drivers a better view of the road and helped reduce blind spots.

Earl was one of the first designers to recognize the importance of aerodynamics in car design. Many of his cars featured streamlined designs that helped reduce wind resistance and improve fuel efficiency. For this reason (as well as for aesthetic reasons), he popularized the idea of cars that were "low and long." All these ideas helped influence the look of American automobiles during the golden age of the 1950s–1970s, which might be summarized by the saying, "Nothing succeeds like excess."

As his biographer, William Knoedelseder, said in an interview, "He had a really good idea of what Americans wanted, and I think he got it growing up in the world where motion pictures were made. He knew what movie stars liked and he knew Americans liked what movie stars liked. Longer. Lower. Wider. Sleeker. That's what he thought cars should be. 'A greyhound,' he used to say, 'is more attractive than a bulldog.'"

While times may have changed, many innovations under Earl's direction still echo down the decades. For example, in place of rear-view mirrors, the 1956 Buick Centurion show car boasted a TV camera that transmitted the rear view to a small screen on the dashboard, anticipating modern car technologies by more than half a century.

HARLEY EARL

Among Earl's most memorable designs are the Chevrolet Nomad, the Cadillac Eldorado Brougham, and the early-1950s Buicks. But perhaps the most iconic car Earl is remembered for is the Chevrolet Corvette. Here, he was influenced by watching cars like the Jaguar and the MG on road-racing courses such as Watkins Glen in New York. Believing America needed its own sports car, he convinced General Motors to develop an affordable two-seater. Earl was involved in its design from the beginning and oversaw the development of the first production models, which were powered by a 150-horsepower, six-cylinder engine and featured a two-speed automatic transmission.

In those days, car manufacturers didn't really have marketing departments, so Earl took control of that too. Recognizing that its sporty styling and high performance would appeal to a younger audience, he promoted the Corvette's sale across a variety of media with the help of A-listers such as Rita Hayworth and Tony Curtis. But he also knew that marketing and design had to work in unison; to an extent, the cars had to sell themselves. As he once noted, "If you go by a school and the kids don't whistle, back to the drawing board."

Below: Cadillac Series 70 Eldorado Brougham

He also liked to keep his employees on their toes. "If a particular group appears to be bogging down over a new fender or grille or interior trim, I sometimes wander into their quarters, make some irrelevant or even zany observation, and then leave," he said. "It is surprising what effect a bit of peculiar behavior will have. First-class minds will seize on anything out of the ordinary and race off, looking for explanations and hidden meanings. That's all I want them to do—start exercising their imaginations. The ideas will soon pop up."

Earl retired in 1958, aged 65. At this point, design had become widely recognized as a leading success factor in car manufacturing. And GM's move to hire the first car designer had paid off handsomely; it had become the biggest corporation in the world. Earl died 11 years later, in 1969, aged 75.

Earl is fondly remembered in the car industry. He was inducted into the Automotive Hall of Fame in 1986, and one of his concept car designs, the Firebird I, is reproduced in miniature on the NASCAR Harley J. Earl Trophy.

"NOTHING SUCCEEDS LIKE EXCESS."
Harley Earl

Above: The 1960 Chevrolet Corvette

DANISH
1894–1967

HIGHLIGHTS
PH three-shade lamps, PH Artichoke lamp, PH 5 lamp

CHARACTERISTICS
Layered shades, functional design, organic forms, affordability

Below: PH 5 Pendant Lamp

POUL HENNINGSEN

"THE TECHNICIAN SHOULD NEVER FORGET THAT HE IS AN ARTIST, THE ARTIST NEVER THAT HE IS A TECHNICIAN."

For many people, an electric light is just something you switch on and off. For the Danish left-wing writer, architect and designer Poul Henningsen, it was something rather more profound. He was fascinated by the ways in which lighting could be used to enhance people's lives, in terms of both their physical comfort and their psychological well-being. And his designs have literally changed the way millions of people look at things for almost a century. To oversimplify things a little (but not overly so), he can essentially be considered the inventor of mood lighting.

Henningsen was born in 1894 in Ordrup, Denmark. He was the fourth child of feminist activist and writer Agnes Henningsen, and the result of an extramarital affair she'd had with satirist Carl Ewald. Henningsen grew up in an unconventional household filled with artistic and intellectual discussions, where major literary and political figures often visited.

Left: Poul Henningsen and Inger F Anderson, 1965

His education and training took place between 1911 and 1917, a time when the world was transitioning from oil lamps to electric light. The story goes that Henningsen's focus on lighting was sparked by his mother, who worried about how she'd look in rooms lit by bright, harsh electric bulbs. Whether or not that story is apocryphal, Henningsen developed a fascination with lighting that dovetailed with his radical leftist desires to improve the living conditions of ordinary people.

Henningsen trained at the Københavns Tekniske Skole (Copenhagen Technical College) and the Danmarks Tekniske Universitet (Technical University of Denmark), where he studied to be an architect but never graduated. After freelancing for a while as an architect, designer, and sometimes writer and journalist, he began designing lamps for Danish lighting manufacturer Louis Poulsen in 1924; their working relationship lasted a lifetime.

Above: The Poul Henningsen room, Danish Museum of Art & Design, Copenhagen, Denmark

It was here that Henningsen achieved his goal of producing an electric lamp that would duplicate the lighting effects of an oil lamp. His groundbreaking PH Lamp employed a series of layered shades that diffused and softened light, eliminated glare, and created a warm and inviting atmosphere. In short, Henningsen had created the first electric-powered "mood lighting," and the world of interior design was changed forever.

The PH Lamp, which is still produced by Louis Poulsen, was also aesthetically distinctive, with a simple, Modernist form that was dramatically different from the ornate fixtures that were standard at the time. And that was no accident, because Henningsen was part of a group of designers, architects, and artists in early 20th-century Denmark who shared a commitment to functionalism in design.

This movement, which became known as the Danish Modern or Scandinavian Modern style, emphasized simplicity, functionality, and a focus on the needs of the user. Henningsen wrote extensively on the subject and believed that good design should be accessible to everyone, not just the wealthy elite.

In 1930 he also reinvented the piano. His revolutionary design of the PH Grand Piano, commissioned for piano manufacturer Andreas Christensen, was a huge departure from the traditional grand piano, stripping things back mercilessly to bring out the beauty of the musical parts. Unique and visionary, the design remains visually surprising to this day.

Above all, Henningsen believed that design should marry form and function harmoniously. As he put it, "The technician should never forget that he is an artist, the artist never that he is a technician." But his activities extended far beyond design. In 1933 he wrote a controversial book, *What About Culture?*, which tore into the snobbishness and conservatism of Danish life. Two years later he released a documentary titled *Danmarksfilmen* (The Film of Denmark), which was blasted by critics but is now considered a classic. Before it could be shown, the government removed 18 scenes and replaced the jazz soundtrack with traditional Danish music. In 1937 he designed his family house in Copenhagen, which he jokingly described as "the ugliest house in Gentofte" due to its radical use of exposed concrete.

In 1940 the Nazis invaded Denmark, and Henningsen, a prominent critic of fascism, had to keep a low profile. In 1943 he fled to neutral Sweden with Jewish architect Arne Jacobsen in a rowing boat. This probably saved his life, as Danish Nazi leader Wilfred Petersen had plotted to kill him and his family by torching their home.

In 1958 Henningsen created his best-known lighting designs. One was the PH Artichoke Pendant, created for the Langelinie Pavilion in Copenhagen. It features a series of overlapping metal "leaves" that combine to evoke a sculptural, organic form. It's a celebrated example of Henningsen's innovative use of layered shades to create visual interest and diffuse light.

He also created the PH 5, a pendant lamp with a distinctive multilayered shade. While many of his earlier designs had been produced in limited quantities and were expensive to manufacture, the PH 5 was designed to be mass-produced and sold at an affordable price. It was hugely popular in Denmark and remains in production today. More broadly, Henningsen's lamp designs eventually became so deeply woven into the fabric of Danish culture that they acquired their own collective noun: PH-lamps.

Throughout his career, Henningsen received numerous awards and honours for his work, including the gold medal at the Milan Triennial in 1954. He continued to design lamps for Louis Poulsen until his death in 1967, and his designs and philosophy of lighting remain popular and influential to this day.

Below: The aptly named PH Artichoke Pendant

HARRY BECK

HIS MOST FAMOUS DESIGN IS STILL USED EVERY SINGLE DAY BY LONDONERS AND VISITORS TO THE CAPITAL OF THE UK.

Harry Beck is mainly known for one thing—but it is a significant one. His London Underground map didn't just make it easy for passengers to find their way around the British capital; it continues to influence transport maps and other wayfinding material around the world.

Beck was born Henry Charles Beck in 1902 in Leyton, east London. His father was a surveyor. By 1911 the Beck family had moved to Highgate, north London, where Harry was educated at Grove House School. He attended art classes locally and studied marble sculpture in Italy. After studying engineering at Leyton Technical Institute, he went to work as a draftsman for the London Underground Signals Office, where he designed signal diagrams.

Signal diagrams are schematics that show the various signals, switches, and other elements of a signalling system and how they are interconnected.

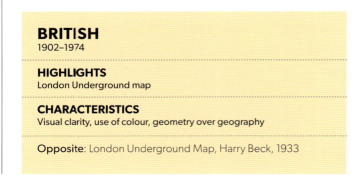

BRITISH
1902–1974

HIGHLIGHTS
London Underground map

CHARACTERISTICS
Visual clarity, use of colour, geometry over geography

Opposite: London Underground Map, Harry Beck, 1933

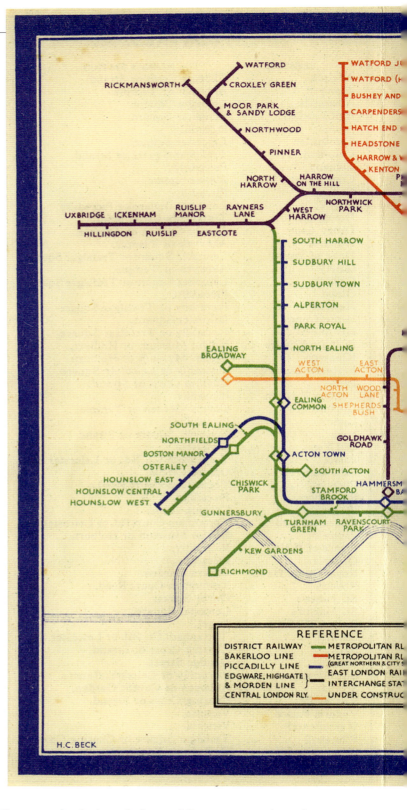

They aren't designed for public consumption, but to help railway engineers and operators plan and maintain the signalling system and troubleshoot problems. Beck had a passion for this work and was particularly interested in the challenge of representing complex information in a clear and intuitive way.

And this led to his masterstroke: applying the design principles of his signal diagrams to a transport map of the Underground stations, and showing how they linked up with each other. Ironically, it was a project he worked on after being laid off from the Signals Office.

Previously, Underground maps had been laid out according to the geography of the stations, often superimposed over a map of the city's roads. Unfortunately, the result was a confusing mess of spaghetti-like lines that was difficult to follow. Beck realized that the travelling public cared less about accurate distances and more about where to change trains to get to where they were going. Designed in 1931, this new map swapped the

29

meandering squiggles of real-life routes for straight lines and 90-degree angles that were not at all geographically accurate, but much easier for commuters to follow. He also gave different lines different colours, so they were easier to track. And while most Underground stations were in reality bunched up together in the centre, Beck's map made them more or less equally spaced so they were easier to distinguish.

Beck submitted his concept to the London Underground in 1931, but it was rejected by the Publicity Office as being too radical. Yet he persisted, and in 1932 they agreed to a trial of 500 copies in selected stations. It was deemed a success, and a pocket version of the map was put into full publication the following year. Despite printing 750,000 copies, it was so popular that they had to do a fresh print run after only one month, and introduce a poster version.

After being made redundant in 1929, Beck was re-employed by London Transport in 1932 as a draftsman and later as a technical editor. In 1938 he produced a diagram of the entire London rail system. He also produced at least one map for British Railways and submitted at least two versions of a diagram for the Paris Métro, although the latter two were rejected. He did freelance design work for other clients too, including the British Electric Traction Company and the Post Office. But Beck became frustrated, as the development of the map was increasingly taken out of his hands; he even threatened legal action. After all, he had never been formally commissioned or paid for the design.

Above: Pocket London Underground Map, 1932

Beck's last version of the map was published in 1960, after which a dispute over its remodelling by other designers led to a major rift with his former employer. Despite this, he continued to work on updated designs, one of which featured the new Victoria Line as a neat diagonal in lilac. This design was, however, never used.

In the mid-1960s, a new generation of writers and graphic designers started to celebrate Beck's map as a design classic. He went on to receive numerous accolades for his work, including an OBE in 1965. He passed away in 1974, but his map lives on. While modifications and additions have been made as the network has evolved, it's broadly the same design today, and is likely to serve the London Underground for decades to come.

In 2020, auctioneer Dominic Winter told the *Daily Mail*, "It's hard to not be captivated by the simple beauty of [Beck's original] design, which quite rightly has stood the test of time as a classic. The colours, the sans font, the abandonment of scale and the straight lines all give it a modern feel. It's been imitated, modified and spoofed countless times over the last 90 years, but Beck's initial design is instantly recognisable in all versions."

It's important not to overstate Beck's contribution to map design. Schematic maps of rail networks existed before his time, as far back as the 19th century. And even most Underground lines displayed schematics that showed the order of stations non-geographically, usually along a single horizontal

"IT'S HARD TO NOT BE CAPTIVATED BY THE SIMPLE BEAUTY OF [BECK'S ORIGINAL] DESIGN, WHICH QUITE RIGHTLY HAS STOOD THE TEST OF TIME AS A CLASSIC."

Dominic Winter

Above: Harry Beck with his map of the London Underground

line. But Beck's Underground map took these principles to a new level by covering an entire city network in a clear and easy-to-follow way. In doing so, he inspired countless others, including Massimo Vignelli's 1972 redesign of the New York City Subway map.

Beck's work is on display in the Beck Gallery at the London Transport Museum in Covent Garden. There are also commemorative plaques at Finchley Central Underground station and his home at 60 Court House Road, Finchley.

MARCEL BREUER

THE ARCHITECT AND DESIGNER REMAINS MUCH ADMIRED.

HUNGARIAN
1902–1981

HIGHLIGHTS
Wassily Chair, Cesca Chair, B5 Chair, African Chair, Slatted Chair

CHARACTERISTICS
Use of tubular steel, minimalist, functional, ergonomic

Above right: Colombo tan leather and chrome armchairs

Marcel Breuer is best known as an architect, but the world of furniture design claims him as one of their own too. A leading figure in the Modernist design movement, Breuer influenced chair design in ways that still reverberate.

He was born in 1902 to a Jewish family in Pécs, Hungary. At 18 he moved to Vienna, where he briefly attended the Akademie der Bildenden Künste Wien (Academy of Fine Arts) in Vienna and trained as a painter. But he hated the atmosphere there. So, after only a year, he dropped out to study at the Bauhaus, a radical arts and crafts school that had only just opened in Weimar, Germany.

Breuer was one of the youngest among the Bauhaus's first intake, but his talent was quickly recognized and he was put in charge of the school's carpentry workshop. During this period he designed

"IT IS INTERESTING THAT THE MODERN FURNITURE WAS PROMOTED NOT BY THE PROFESSIONAL FURNITURE DESIGNERS, BUT BY THE ARCHITECTS."

Marcel Breuer

his now-celebrated African Chair (a collaboration with fellow student Gunta Stölzl in 1921) and his Slatted Chair (1922), an elastic, inclined seat with elastic rear belts designed to promote a comfortable and ergonomic seated posture.

Later, after the school moved from Weimar to Dessau, Breuer began teaching at its newly established department of architecture. But he didn't lose interest in furniture. And in 1925, inspired by the design of an Adler bicycle's handlebars, he created the first tubular metal chair.

Made of curving tubes of steel and leather slings, the Model B3 chair took advantage of the latest manufacturing innovations and looked nothing like what people expected a chair to look like at the time. It was named Wassily by an Italian manufacturer who'd heard that Wassily Kandinsky (another teacher at the Bauhaus) had admired it, and that Breuer had made one for him as a gift.

Inspired by the Constructivist principles of De Stijl (a modern art movement that grew out of the Netherlands in the early 20th century), its design stripped back the concept of a chair to its bare essentials. But at the same time it was highly ergonomic and comfortable, fitting in perfectly with the principles of the International Style.

Closely related to Modernism, the International Style developed in design and architecture in the 1920s and 1930s. Its characteristics include the use of lightweight, mass-produced industrial materials; rejection of all ornament and colour; repetitive modular forms; and the use of flat surfaces, often alternating with glass.

Breuer also attracted attention for the B32 chair, aka the Cesca Chair (named after his daughter, Francesca). Designed in 1926, it was a cantilevered chair made with a tubular steel frame that was bent into shape. In this way, it cleverly combined traditional craftsmanship (woven caning hand-sewn into the wood frame) with the methods of industrial mass production (used to manipulate the tubular steel).

He went on to design a whole range of furniture constructed around tubular metal, including chairs, tables, stools, and cupboards. He liked the material because it was clean, affordable, could be designed with clear geometric lines, and offered comfort without the need for springs.

Before leaving the Bauhaus in 1928, he designed the interiors and furnishings for the masters' houses there. This included the B5 chair (designed in 1926 and manufactured in 1927). Made of nickel-plated tubular steel, it was manufactured by Breuer's own company, which became a bone of contention with Bauhaus founder Walter Gropius, a German-American architect who expected everything at the school to be made in-house.

The Bauhaus closed in 1933 and, as a Jew, Breuer eventually had no choice but to leave Germany for London. While there, he was employed at Isokon, a company founded by Jack Pritchard and Wells Coates that designed and constructed Modernist houses and flats, as well as furniture and fittings for them, under the influence of Russian Constructivism.

During this period Breuer designed his Long Chair and experimented with bent and formed plywood inspired by the designs by Finnish architect Alvar Aalto. Between 1935 and 1937 he designed a number of houses in collaboration with English Modernist F.R.S. Yorke. Then, after a brief time as Isokon's head of design, in 1937 he accepted an invitation from

Above: Chaise Longue, 1938, MOMA, The Museum of Modern Art, New York City, USA

MARCEL BREUER

Above: Bauhaus design interior exterior, Dessau, Germany, with chair B3 in foreground

Gropius to teach at Harvard University in the United States.

The two men formed a partnership that was to greatly influence the American approach to designing modern houses. An iconic example of their furniture and interior-design work during this period is the Alan I W Frank House in Pittsburgh, designed as a Gesamtkunstwerk, or "total work of art." The two split, however, in 1941, after Breuer married their secretary, Constance Crocker Leighton. Breuer moved to New York in 1946, with Harry Seidler as his chief draftsman, and became a naturalized American citizen in 1944.

Breuer's architectural practice in the US lasted from 1946 to 1976 and produced more than 100 buildings, including the Frank House (1940), the Whitney Museum of American Art (1966), and the UNESCO Headquarters (1952–58). He died in 1981, aged 79.

In terms of his legacy, the Brutalist style he championed in some of his larger projects remains controversial. In contrast, his furniture designs have remained near-universally popular. Not only are they regarded as icons of Modernist design, but both his Wassily Chair and Cesca Chair remain in production, as well as inspiring countless copies.

TELEGRAMS AND CABLES:　　　　　　TELEPHONE:
PENGUINOOK, WEST DRAYTON　　　　　　　　　　SKYPORT 1984 (7 LINES)

PENGUIN　　BOOKS LTD

HARMONDSWORTH · MIDDLESEX

DIRECTORS: SIR ALLEN LANE · RICHARD LANE · SIR WILLIAM EMRYS WILLIAMS, C.B.E.
EUNICE FROST, O.B.E. · H. F. PAROISSIEN · HANS SCHMOLLER

ELIZABETH FRIEDLÄNDER

"AS YOU ARE A NON-ARYAN AND AS SUCH YOU LACK THE NECESSARY RELIABILITY AND FITNESS TO PARTICIPATE IN THE CREATION AND DISSEMINATION OF GERMAN CULTURAL VALUES. I, THEREFORE, FORBID YOU TO CONTINUE TO PRACTISE YOUR PROFESSION AS A GRAPHIC DESIGNER."

Professional Union of German Industrial Graphic Designers

GERMAN
1903–1984

HIGHLIGHTS
Bookwork, calligraphy, decorative designs

CHARACTERISTICS
Hand-drawn, colourful, technically exacting

Opposite: Friedländer's exceptional design for Penguin Books' 25th anniversary

Born in Germany in 1903, Elisabeth Friedländer was a pioneer in an era when few women were accepted into the design profession. That in itself would be notable enough, but the twists and turns in her life and work make her story even more fascinating.

She was born in Berlin to a wealthy and cultured Jewish family. After studying typography and calligraphy under German painter and graphic artist E.R. Weiss at the Berlin Academy, she worked as a designer and calligrapher for the fashion magazine *Die Dame* (*The Woman*). This attracted the attention of Georg Hartmann of the Bauer Type Foundry in Frankfurt, and in 1928 he commissioned her to design a typeface.

The typeface was originally named Friedlander-Antiqua, but the rise of Hitler led to them to retitle it Elisabeth-Antiqua (spelled "Elizabeth" in some countries), because Friedländer was a recognizably Jewish name. Characterized by grace, elegance, and subtle influences from both classic and contemporary typography, Elisabeth-Antiqua was popular for decades among book publishers, particularly private presses that wished to give a refined air to their designs. It was revived in 2005 by Spanish type designer Andreu Balius in a digital version that includes most glyphs of the original.

By the time the typeface was first cut in 1938, however, Friedländer had long left Germany. In 1936 she had been denied membership in the Professional Union of German Industrial Graphic Designers. They wrote to her, "As you are a non-Aryan and as such you lack the necessary reliability and fitness to participate in the creation and dissemination of German cultural values. I, therefore, forbid you to continue to practise your profession as a graphic designer."

Above: The Elisabeth-Antiqua font, designed by Friedänder

Shortly afterwards, she moved to Milan. There, she spent two years working for the publisher Mondadori and attempting to secure a US visa, having been offered a job by Bauer Type Foundry, which had opened a New York office. Although she had received recommendations from Italian conductor Arturo Toscanini, publishing company Random House and English playwright and composer Noël Coward, her efforts were unsuccessful. And then, in 1939, Italy passed anti-Jewish laws, and Friedländer was again forced to leave.

She moved to London in 1939 on a domestic-service visa arranged by the Religious Society of Friends, aka Quakers, who were active in helping Jewish refugees. She arrived in Britain carrying little but two portfolios of work and an early-18th-century Klotz violin that had belonged to her mother.

In Britain she anglicized her name to Elizabeth Friedlander and was released from servitude thanks to the poet and printer Francis Meynell; he introduced her to author Ellic Howe, who was at that time working for the Political Warfare Executive, a government department engaged in "black propaganda" against Germany. She worked there for the rest of the war, using her design skills to forge identity papers, ration books, and Wehrmacht and Nazi rubber stamps.

After the war she decided to stay in Britain. She became a naturalized citizen and worked with fellow refugee Jan Tschichold at Penguin doing pattern designs for book covers—notably for pocket-sized paperbacks of classical-music scores. She continued to work with Penguin for many years, as well as getting commissions from a wide range of other clients.

Notable projects included her advertising work for cosmetics brands; decorative borders for Linotype; printer's flowers for Monotype; calligraphy for the Roll of Honour at Sandhurst; a logo for Penguin; book designs for Mills & Boon, Reader's Digest, Mondadori, and Thames & Hudson; and literary and art projects for Curwen Press. She showed no interest in returning to her homeland. In 1959, in a reply to a job offer in Germany, she wrote, "One simply cannot go back when one left so long ago. Too much has happened in-between and the old homeland has become alien and I have found a home in a new land."

Above: The Shell Petroleum Company were among Friedländer's many commissions

Above: Samples of the beautiful patterns that Elizabeth Friedländer designed

She left London in the early 1960s to live in Cork, Ireland with the Irish-Italian writer and professor Alessandro Magri MacMahon. He had been driven out of Italy because of his anti-fascist activities, and they'd met through her wartime work for the British government. Once settled, she formed a circle of artistic friends including writers Elizabeth Bowen and Molly Keane.

Despite her failing eyesight, Friedländer continued working until her death in 1984.

She left her archive and her mother's violin to her friend Sheila Goldberg, the wife of Gerald Goldberg, who became the first Jewish lord mayor of Cork. They later donated both to the Cork School of Music, which loans the violin to an outstanding pupil every year.

While many of her designs were instantly recognizable to audiences of the 20th century, Friedländer's own story was little known, partly because she was reluctant to speak about her personal life. In recent years, however, that has changed.

In 2016 Katharine Meynell, granddaughter of Francis Meynell, wrote and produced *Elisabeth*, a short film about Friedländer's life and work. And two years later Meynell curated the first public exhibition devoted entirely to Friedländer's work at the Ditchling Museum of Art + Craft in East Sussex. The show highlighted the wide variety of her output, featuring everything from book covers and end papers to wood engravings, greeting cards, illustrated maps, and type specimens as well as her commercial work, including technical drawings for cosmetics.

"I HAVE FOUND A HOME IN A NEW LAND."

Elizabeth Friedländer

JACQUELINE GROAG

HER BEAUTIFUL TEXTILE DESIGNS WERE WORN BY ROYALTY AND LOVED BY BRITISH WOMEN, LEAVING A LASTING LEGACY OF INFLUENCE ON MODERN DESIGNERS.

CZECH
1903–1986

HIGHLIGHTS
Textile design, interior design

CHARACTERISTICS
Childlike simplicity, bold colours, use of grids

Opposite: Dresses made in Groag's distinctive patterns

Jacqueline Groag was arguably the most influential textile designer in post-war Britain. And yet she was neither British nor called Jacqueline. In fact, she was born Hilde Pick in Prague in 1903.

Growing up in an affluent Jewish family, Groag was plagued by ill health and so, unlike her siblings, she was largely home-schooled. She was also quite a solitary child who spent time alone drawing. Later in life, she shared a theory that everyone has a particular age that they remain inside, regardless of their real age; hers was eight. This outlook was reflected in her pattern designs, which benefit from a childlike simplicity that is typically colourful, beautifully balanced, and structurally elegant.

In the 1920s, she studied textile design in Vienna under the tutelage of Austrian painter Franz Cizek, who suggested that she concentrate on surface design. In general, he urged his students to set aside their formal teaching in favour of a less structured approach. Given her home-schooling and lack of exams, this was pushing against an open door for Groag.

Cizek then recommended her to Josef Hoffmann, head of the Wiener Werkstätte (Vienna Workshop), which brought together architects, artists, designers and artisans working in ceramics, fashion, silver,

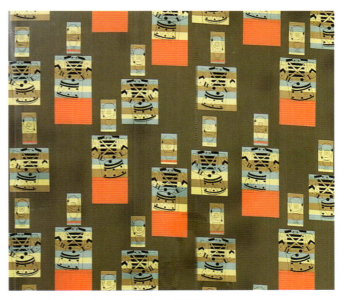

Above: Toy Parade dress design, 1955

furniture, and the graphic arts. Groag became one of Hoffmann's students at the Kunstgewerbeschule (School of Arts and Crafts) and managed to sell designs to the Werkstätte while still a student, as well as winning prizes for her work. This included first prize for a poster design for the Salzburg Festival in the 1920s.

Her work often centred around a grid, where squares were filled with drawings of things like figures, animals, and abstract motifs. This stood in stark contrast to the ethos of the International Modernist movement, which eschewed decoration as frivolous and unnecessary. After graduation she became an active participant in the Wiener Werkstätte; the progressive group sought ways of embedding artistry and individuality into everyday design.

Groag went to Paris in 1929, and by the following year she was already designing textiles for Coco Chanel and Elsa Schiaparelli, who between them dominated fashion during the interwar period. Her 1938 First Night dress print for Schiaparelli was based on her drawing of the audience during opening night at the Paris Opera. The fabric was sold in the United States under the name Gala Night.

She also worked for other celebrated French couturiers including Lanvin, the House of Worth, and Paul Poiret. Her work won a series of awards, including one for a lace design at the Paris Colonial Exposition in 1931, a gold medal at the Milan Triennial in 1933, and a gold medal for textiles at the 1937 Paris Exposition.

She changed her name to Jacqueline Groag after marrying Jacques Groag in 1937 following a long engagement. She'd first met the Modernist artist and fellow Czech at the beginning of the decade at a Viennese masked ball. In 1938, following the Anschluss (the Nazi unification of Austria and Germany), the couple fled Vienna for Britain. They were met in London by leading members of the British Design Factory, including Sir Gordon Russell, Sir Charles Reilly and Jack Pritchard.

During the 1940s Groag designed a wide range of dress fabrics for calico printing company F.W. Grafton. One of her patterns, a classic tulip motif, was chosen by British couturier Edward Molyneux for a dress he designed for HRH Princess Elizabeth in 1946. Groag and her husband gained British citizenship in 1947. In 1948 *The Ambassador* magazine drew attention to her sheer versatility. "Few designers can move easily from abstract design to the representational and produce equally good work in both disciplines,"

Above: King George VI and Princess Elizabeth wearing one of Groag's designs, 1946

Below: First Night dress print for Schiaparelli, based on her drawing of the opening night at the Paris Opera

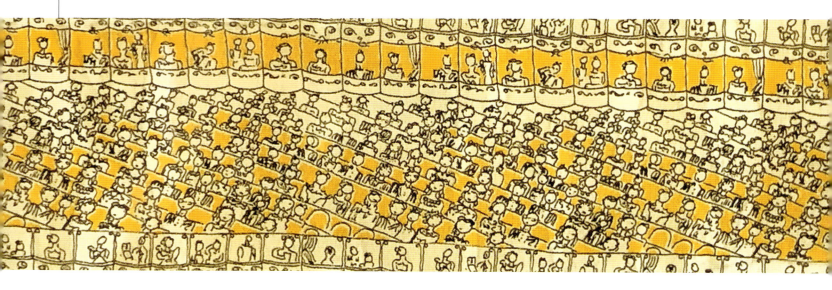

JACQUELINE GROAG

"FEW DESIGNERS CAN MOVE EASILY FROM ABSTRACT DESIGN TO THE REPRESENTATIONAL AND PRODUCE EQUALLY GOOD WORK IN BOTH DISCIPLINES."

The Ambassador magazine

it stated. "Jacqueline Groag not only possesses this special gift but also the ability to abstract from life so that reality still exists in many of her patterns, but transformed by the wit and charm of her own personality."

Groag and her husband became members of the Society of Industrial Artists, and by the 1950s she'd established a strong reputation as a designer for the British textile industry. Her contribution to the 1951 Festival of Britain turned many heads; it was a curtain of simulated threaded bones for the Dome of Discovery's Living World exhibition.

Over time her work grew in stature and became a major influence on pattern design around the world. Some of her most celebrated designs include silkscreen motifs for dinnerware made by Johnson Matthey, and her amorphic printed patterns for textile company David Whitehead & Sons. She worked for a range of noteworthy clients including Associated American Artists, Hallmark Cards, and John Lewis.

In the 1960s and 1970s Groag became more involved with the interiors of boats, aircraft, and trains. She worked on the design of textiles and plastics for British Overseas Airways Corporation and British Rail, and was commissioned by designer Misha Black in the 1970s to make a moquette for London Transport; it was used for seating on buses and Tube trains. She was appointed a Royal Designer for Industry in 1984, an honour given by the Royal Society of Arts to a select few who have achieved "sustained excellence in aesthetic and efficient design for industry." She died, aged 82, on 13 January 1986.

Right: Puppet Ballet print, 1953

CHARLOTTE PERRIAND

SHE IS RENOWNED AS ONE OF THE MOST INFLUENTIAL FURNITURE DESIGNERS OF THE EARLY MODERN MOVEMENT.

"THE EXTENSION OF THE ART OF DWELLING IS THE ART OF LIVING."

FRENCH
1903–1999

HIGHLIGHTS
Le Bar sous le Toit, B301 Chair, LC2 Chair, B306 Chaise Longue

CHARACTERISTICS
Democratic approach, focus on affordability and durability, machine aesthetic (early work), natural materials (later work)

Opposite: Maison du Mexique bookcase

Charlotte Perriand was driven by the idea that good design should be accessible to everyone, because it makes for a better society. And she didn't just pay lip service to that notion. Instead, her practice was firmly focused on developing functional furniture for the masses.

She was born in Paris to a tailor father and a seamstress mother. After being praised at school for her art skills, she enrolled in the École de l'Union Centrale des Arts Décoratifs (School of the Central Union of Decorative Arts) in 1920 to study furniture design. Her teachers there included Henri Rapin, a painter, illustrator, and interior designer famed for his role in the Art Deco movement.

After graduating, Perriand continued to study by taking part in workshops and lectures organized by department stores, notably with Maurice Dufrêne of La Maîtrise furniture workshop. She was fascinated by the notion of transforming people's environments into somewhere more beautiful and functional.

Two years after graduating, she renovated her own apartment with light-reflecting aluminium and nickel-plated surfaces teamed with leather cushions and glass shelves. Her interior also featured a built-in wall bar made of aluminium, glass, and chrome, and a card table with built-in pool-pocket drink holders. She recreated this design as *Bar sous le Toit* (*Bar under the Roof*) at the 1927 Salon d'Automne, an annual art exhibition held in Paris.

Perriand won praise for her work, but she didn't just want to create designs for the wealthy. In this, she was inspired by Swiss-French architect Le Corbusier, who believed in providing better living conditions for people in crowded cities. She even applied to work at his studio. However, at the interview, he took one brief glance at her drawings before dismissing her with the comment, "We don't embroider cushions here."

She left her card with Le Corbusier anyway, and later that year invited him to see her installation at Salon d'Automne. He was so impressed, he offered her a job at his studio. Perriand stayed there from 1927 to 1937, taking charge of the studio's interiors work and promoting its designs through a series of exhibitions. During this period, she worked alongside Swiss architect Pierre Jeanneret and collaborated with some of the biggest artists of the time, including Fernand Léger, Pablo Picasso, and Alexander Calder.

In 1928 she designed three chairs made from tubular steel frames based on Le Corbusier's axiom that the chair was a "machine for sitting." At the latter's request, one was made for conversation (the B301 Sling Back Chair), another for relaxation (the LC2 Grand Comfort Chair), and the last for sleeping (the B306 Chaise Longue). The following year she created a model modern apartment in glass and tubular steel to be exhibited as *Équipement d'Habitation* (*Living Equipment*) at Salon d'Automne.

In the 1930s Perriand became involved with a number of leftist organizations, including the Association des Écrivains et Artistes Révolutionnaires and Maison de la Culture, and travelled to Moscow twice for architectural conferences. In her design work she became more egalitarian, moving away from expensive materials such as chrome and toward more affordable materials such as wood and cane. Many of her designs from this time were inspired by the handcrafted furniture of Savoie, in southeastern France, where her paternal grandparents lived and where she had often visited as a child.

After parting ways with Le Corbusier in 1937, she collaborated with Léger on a pavilion for the 1937 Paris Exposition and worked on a ski resort in Savoie. Then, as war was breaking out, she went to work for Jean Prouvé, a self-taught architect and

Left: The 1928 dining room

Above right: Charlotte Perriand: Inventing a New World exhibition at the Paris Fondation Louis Vuitton Museum, 2019, Paris, France

CHARLOTTE PERRIAND

she saw a retrospective of her work exhibited at the Musée des Arts Décoratifs in Paris. Then, in 1998, a further retrospective took place at the Design Museum in London, to accompany publication of her autobiography, *Une Vie de Création*.

She died one year later, aged 96. But her name continues to play a role in design through the Charlotte Perriand Award. Part of The Créateurs Design Association & Awards, the peer-to-peer program aims to highlight extraordinary work in interior design, product design, and architecture. Just as influential, though, is the distinct philosophy Perriand expounded and practised. As she wrote in 1981, "The extension of the art of dwelling is the art of living—living in harmony with man's deepest drives and with his adopted or fabricated environment."

designer whose career spanned architectural design, industrial design, structural design, and furniture design. She began by designing metal objects such as screens and stair railings, then the war shifted their focus towards military barracks and furnishings for temporary housing.

When France fell to the Nazis in 1940, Perriand went to Japan to work as an official adviser for industrial design to the Ministry for Trade and Industry. In 1942 she was forced to leave the country as an "illegal alien," but on her way back to Europe she was caught in a naval blockade and forced into exile in Vietnam. During her time there she studied woodwork and weaving, and investigated the principles of Eastern design inspired by a 1906 essay by Okakura Kakuzō: *The Book of Tea: A Japanese Harmony of Art, Culture and the Simple Life*.

After returning to Paris in 1946, Perriand began collaborating on design work with Prouvé. Other notable projects over the next three decades included her remodelling of Air France's offices in London, Paris, and Tokyo; The League of Nations building for the United Nations in Geneva; and the Méribel ski resort in the French Alps. In 1985, at the age of 82,

Below: Charlotte Perriand lamp in bedroom with earth walls, terracotta floor and traditional berber wood ceiling

EVA ZEISEL

"BEAUTIFUL THINGS MAKE PEOPLE HAPPY."
Eva Zeisel

HUNGARIAN
1906–2011

HIGHLIGHTS
Ceramics

CHARACTERISTICS
Organic, sensuous forms, use of bird themes, functional and modular approach

Left: Gobelin 8, tea service, 1929

Opposite: Silhouette glass pattern

For some people, work is a chore and retirement cannot come soon enough. For Eva Zeisel, work was a joy. Thankfully, she was able to carry on designing ceramics right up till her death at 105, and her work remains highly collectable. And yet, given the turbulent nature of her early life, it could have all turned out very different.

She was born in Budapest, Hungary, in 1906 to a wealthy Jewish family. Her mother, Laura Polányi, later Striker, was a historian and the first woman to get a PhD from the University of Budapest. Zeisel's uncles were also well known in intellectual circles: Karl Polányi as a sociologist and economist, and Michael Polányi as a chemist and philosopher of science.

Zeisel, in contrast, was attracted to art. At 17 she went to study at Budapest's Magyar Képzőművészeti Akadémia (Hungarian Royal Academy of Fine Arts). She was a keen painter, but her mother urged her to find a more stable way to earn a living, so she apprenticed herself to Jakob Karapancsik, the last pottery master from the medieval guild system. Under his tutelage, she learned ceramics and became the first woman to qualify as a journeyman in the Hungarian Guild of Chimney Sweeps, Oven Makers, Roof Tilers, Well Diggers, and Potters.

After graduating, Zeisel found work at the Hansa-Kunst-Keramik, a ceramic workshop in Hamburg. She took the position, she later said, "because it was the furthest from home." She then got a job as a designer in the Black Forest region of Germany, where she worked for about two years creating geometric designs for dinnerware, tea sets, vases, inkwells, and other ceramic items.

In 1930 Zeisel moved to Berlin and worked designing for one of the pottery factories owned by the Carstens family. During this time she met physicist Alexander Weissberg, and they became engaged in 1932. That same year, they followed the example of many other young artists and intellectuals and visited the Soviet Union to learn about the new social and artistic movements developing there. She was offered a position assisting in the modernization of the ceramic industry and she accepted it with enthusiasm.

Zeisel travelled across Russia for the role and was eventually promoted to artistic director for the Porcelain and Glass Industries for the entire USSR. In 1936, however, her fortunes reversed; she was accused of plotting against Stalin, placed in solitary confinement for 18 months, and subjected to brainwashing and torture. These experiences inspired a famous Hungarian novel, *Darkness at Noon*, written by her friend Arthur Koestler in 1940.

The reason for her imprisonment was never spelled out, and neither was her exoneration; suddenly she was released without explanation and put on a train to Austria. The country was, however, about to be annexed by Nazi Germany (known as the Anschluss) and was not a safe place for a Jew. Zeisel travelled on to England, where her fiancé was waiting for her, and they finally married. In 1937 they settled permanently in the US.

Zeisel began her American career by teaching at the Pratt Institute in New York. She also collaborated with one of her students, Frances Blod, to create designs for the Bay Ridge Specialty Company, including Stratoware, a rare, short-lived line made for Sears.

In 1942 Zeisel was commissioned by the Museum of Modern Art (MoMA) and Castleton China to design a set of modern porcelain dishware that would be worthy of exhibition, and produced for sale by Castleton. *New Shapes in Modern China Designed by Eva Zeisel* ran in 1946, and was the first one-woman exhibition at MoMA. It received critical praise, but because of wartime constraints, the china did not go into production until 1949.

Once it did, her dishes, known as Museum and Castleton White, were popular and continued to be manufactured and sold over several decades—initially in white, and later with a variety of decorations. Zeisel credited the commission with establishing her in the US, saying, "It made me an accepted first-rate designer rather than a run-of-the-mill designer."

Above: Stacked white vases designed for KleinReid shown at her home in New York City, 2004

She went on to design for Hall China, Red Wing China, Norleans Meito (Japan), Western Stoneware, Hyalyn, Philipp Rosenthal (Germany), Mancioli (Italy), Federal Glass, Heisey Glass, Noritake (Japan), Nikkon Toki (Japan), and others.

The distinguishing characteristic of her work was an organic approach to Modernism that incorporated sensuous forms, often inspired by the curves of the human body. She told the New York Sun, "I don't create angular things. I'm a more circular person—it's more my character… even the air between my hands is round." She was also known for her use of bird themes, which echoed the Hungarian folk arts of her childhood.

More fundamentally, Zeisel was focused not on making artistic objects to be stared at in galleries but functional, modular designs that served a purpose for individuals and families, and saved space in the

"I'M A MORE CIRCULAR PERSON—IT'S MORE MY CHARACTER… EVEN THE AIR BETWEEN MY HANDS IS ROUND."

Eva Zeisel

home. Ironic, then, that her work has become highly collectable. Among the most in-demand items are her biomorphic Town and Country dishes, produced by Red Wing Pottery in 1947 as part of a set that included her "mother and child" salt and pepper shakers.

In the 1960s and 1970s, Zeisel left design to work on American history writing projects. She researched the New York Conspiracy, an alleged slave rebellion in 1741 that resulted in many innocent people being put to death or transported to the Caribbean. Zeisel found parallels between their experiences and her own during Stalin's show trials.

She returned to design in the 1980s, a decade in which a 50-year retrospective of her work travelled across the US, Europe, and Russia. Notable works since then include glassware, ceramics, furniture, and lamps for The Orange Chicken; porcelain, crystal, and limited-edition prints for KleinReid; glasses and giftware for Nambé; rugs for The Rug Company; and Classic Century, a best-selling dinnerware range produced by Royal Stafford for Crate & Barrel. She also sold furniture and gifts under her own brand, Eva Zeisel Originals, where Classic Century can currently be found.

In 2005, Zeisel won a Lifetime Achievement Award from Cooper Hewitt, Smithsonian Design Museum. She also received the two highest civilian awards from the Hungarian government as well as the Pratt Institute's Legends Award and awards from the Industrial Designers Society of America and Alfred University. She was an honorary member of the Royal Society of Industrial Designers, and received honorary degrees from the Parsons School of Design (The New School), Rhode Island School of Design, the Royal College of Art, and the Hungarian University of the Arts.

Today her works can be found in the permanent collections of the Metropolitan Museum of Art, the Brooklyn Museum, Cooper Hewitt, MoMA, the British Museum, the Victoria and Albert Museum, and the Bröhan Museum in Berlin, among many others.

Above: Tomorrow's Classic coffee pot, gravy boat and saucer

AMERICAN
1907–1978 / 1912–1988

HIGHLIGHTS
Eames Lounge Chair,
Dining Chair Wood,
Dining Chair Metal

CHARACTERISTICS
Handcrafting, traditional techniques, natural motifs, geometric shapes and patterns

Right: Wirework chair

Opposite: Hang It All coat rack

CHARLES AND RAY EAMES

"RECOGNIZING THE NEED IS THE PRIMARY CONDITION FOR DESIGN."

Charles Eames

Charles and Ray Eames were a married couple of industrial designers who made significant historical contributions to the development of both architecture and furniture through the work of their company, the Eames Office. They also worked in the fields of industrial and graphic design, fine art, and film. Each was a great designer in their own right, but they were very much a team, and it makes sense to treat them as a single entry on our list.

Charles Ormond Eames Jr. was born in St. Louis in 1907; his father was a railway security officer. He developed an early interest in architecture and photography, and won a scholarship to study architecture at the Sam Fox School of Design & Visual Arts at Washington University. However, he left after two years following a series of disagreements with his tutors about modern architecture.

In 1930, aged 23, he began his own architectural practice in St. Louis with partner Charles Gray. He was greatly influenced by Finnish architect Eliel Saarinen, whose son, Eero, later became a partner and friend. In 1938, at Saarinen senior's invitation, Eames moved to Michigan with his first wife and daughter to further study architecture at the Cranbrook Academy of Art in Bloomfield Hills. He became an instructor and the head of the industrial-design department.

Together with Eero Saarinen, Eames entered the Museum of Modern Art's Organic Design in Home Furnishings competition by designing prize-winning furniture. It was during this project that he met Ray Kaiser; she was a student at Cranbrook, and helped with graphic design.

Ray had been born Bernice Alexandra Kaiser in 1912, in Sacramento, California. Her father managed a vaudeville theatre until 1920, when he became an insurance salesman. In 1933, Kaiser graduated from Bennett College in Millbrook, New York, where her art teacher was Lu Duble. She moved to New York City to study abstract expressionist painting with Duble's mentor, the German-American artist Hans Hofmann.

In 1936 Kaiser became a founding member of the American Abstract Artists group, which promoted abstract art at a time when major galleries refused to show it. She became a key figure in the New York art scene and made friends with abstract expressionists Lee Krasner and Mercedes Matter.

"TAKE YOUR PLEASURE SERIOUSLY."
Charles Eames

Left: The highly recognizable Eames Leather chair lounge and ottoman footstool

Sadly, most of her art from this period has been lost, but one of her lithographs is in the permanent collection of the Whitney Museum of American Art.

In 1940 she went to study at Cranbrook at the suggestion of her architect friend Ben Baldwin. It was there that she expanded her skillset and interests to other art and design pursuits beyond painting and, as mentioned, met Charles Eames.

Charles was married at the time, but he divorced in early 1941 and married Ray later that year. The couple moved to Los Angeles and began a hugely successful and influential career in design and architecture. Their design studio, the Eames Office, was based in the Venice area of the city, and operated from 1943 to 1988. The couple worked 13-hour days, six or seven days a week, and directed a team of designers including Gregory Ain, Don Albinson, Harry Bertoia, Annette Del Zoppo, Peter Jon Pearce, and Deborah Sussman.

One of their earliest projects was a leg splint they developed for wounded soldiers during World War II. They were fashioned from wood veneers bonded together with a resin glue, and shaped into compound curves using a process involving heat and pressure. The new plywood design replaced metal traction splints, which were known to induce gangrene by impairing blood circulation.

The US Navy's funding for the splints allowed the couple to experiment more heavily with furniture design and mass production. Among the many important designs they developed were the moulded-plywood DCW (Dining Chair Wood) and DCM (Dining Chair Metal, with a plywood seat) (1945), the Eames Lounge Chair (1956), the Aluminum Group (1958), the Eames Chaise (1968), and the Solar Do-Nothing Machine (1957), an early solar-energy experiment for the Aluminum Company of America.

Above: The Eames DCW dining chair

The best known of all of these was probably the Eames Lounge Chair. Designed in 1956 for Herman Miller, its story began when Ray and Charles visited British director, screenwriter, and producer Billy Wilder, known for movies including *Some Like It Hot* and *The Seven Year Itch*. After watching Wilder try to nap on makeshift lounge chairs in between takes, the couple was inspired to create a chair that

CHARLES AND RAY EAMES

combined the looks of an old English club chair with, in Charles's words, "the warm, receptive look of a well-used first baseman's mitt."

Charles and Ray, determined to maximize comfort and realize their aesthetic vision, created what is essentially a functional work of art. Made of moulded plywood and leather, the seat of the Eames Lounge Chair is permanently tilted at a 15-degree angle. This takes weight off the lower spine and distributes it to the back of the chair, while the lower back is supported by cushions. Besides being comfortable, the design helps restore normal circulation after a long work day.

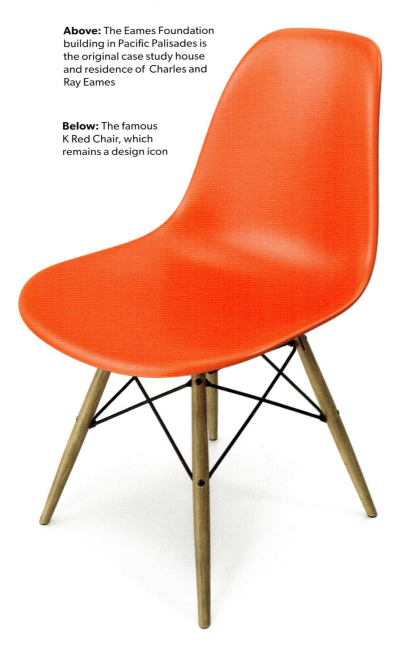

Above: The Eames Foundation building in Pacific Palisades is the original case study house and residence of Charles and Ray Eames

Below: The famous K Red Chair, which remains a design icon

The chair has evolved in various ways, but it remains in production. The couple's best-known design, it is part of the permanent collection at the Museum of Modern Art and has inspired a whole industry of ergonomic furniture design. However, in terms of the Eameses' output, it's somewhat of an outlier in being produced for the luxury-price end of the market. In general, their interest was in producing mass-market furniture that was affordable, albeit still high in quality.

The Eameses conceived and designed a number of exhibitions as well as working on a number of architectural projects, although many never came to fruition. The couple also had a strong interest in photography and theatre, and were involved in the production of 125 short films. Some documented their interests, such as collecting toys and cultural artifacts on their travels; some captured the process of hanging their exhibits or producing furniture designs. Others were more artistic and experimental. *Powers of Ten*, for example, demonstrates the concept of orders of magnitude by visually zooming away from the earth to the edge of the universe, and zooming into a carbon atom. This became an influential technique adopted by many Hollywood filmmakers.

Charles died in 1978, aged 71, while Ray survived a further decade, passing away in 1988 at the age of 75. Charles' daughter, Lucia, spent the final years of her life planning the continuation of the Eames legacy, and founded the Eames Foundation in 2004. In 2008, the US Postal Service released a set of 16 stamps celebrating the couple's designs, and their work has continued to be celebrated in exhibitions across the globe.

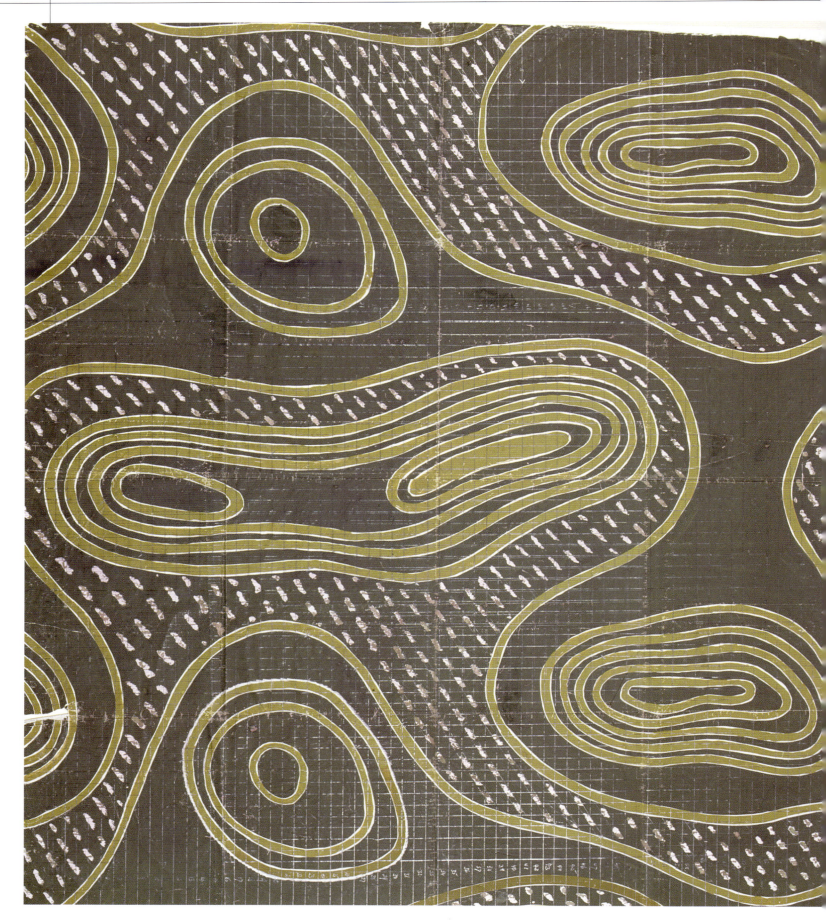

MARIANNE STRAUB

STRAUB WAS ONE OF THE LEADING COMMERCIAL DESIGNERS OF TEXTILES IN BRITAIN FROM THE 1940S TO THE 1960S.

SWISS
1909–1994

HIGHLIGHTS
Textile design

CHARACTERISTICS
Use of hand-weaving, bright colours, strong fabrics

Opposite: The 1951 Surrey design pattern

Creating upholstery for everything from London's Underground to British European Airways (BEA), Marianne Straub was a strong proponent of mass production. And yet she typically created her designs on a handloom first, believing this was the best way to achieve quality results.

Straub was born in the village of Amriswil, Switzerland, the second of four daughters of a textile merchant. As a child, she spent over four years in hospital after contracting tuberculosis, coming home at the age of eight. She went on to study art at Zurich's Kunstgewerbeschule (School of Arts and Crafts). In her last two years, she specialized in hand-weaving and textiles under Heinz Otto Hürlimann, who had studied weaving at the Bauhaus.

At that time, Swiss technical colleges refused to accept female students. Consequently, Straub spent six months working as a technician at a mill in her village before coming to England in 1932 to spend a year studying at Bradford Technical College. She was the only woman attending at the time, and the third in the history of the college. The course covered textile maths, weaving technology, and raw materials as well as cloth construction, and she developed skills in double-cloth textile construction and the

Above: Artists Village Show, Great Bardfield, Essex, with Straub third from left

use of power looms. An experimenter at heart, Straub used vegetable dyes in her fabrication and explored materials such as bamboo, mica, metal, fibreglass, cellophane, and paper yarns.

After graduating from Bradford, she went to work for celebrated British hand-loom weaver Ethel Mairet at her home and workshop, Gospels, in Ditchling, East Sussex. She was introduced to spinning, natural dyeing, and the English Arts and Crafts tradition, and the two developed a deep friendship.

Straub later began working as a peripatetic design consultant for the Welsh milling industry, advising 72 mills that were supported by the Rural Industries Bureau between 1934 and 1937 and learning the skills of mass production. "I decided early in my art school period that I wanted to become a designer in industry," she said. "I wanted to design things which people who were not rich could afford."

In 1937 Straub joined Helios, a subsidiary of cotton spinners Barlow & Jones, as head designer. There, she worked on a dobby loom and was responsible for major advances in fabric production on power looms as well as setting a precedent for hand weaves for mass production. She became managing director in 1947.

In 1950 she went to work for textiles manufacturer Warner & Sons. One of her popular early designs for them was the Surrey, a textile that was used in the interiors of the Regatta Restaurant at the 1951 Festival of Britain.

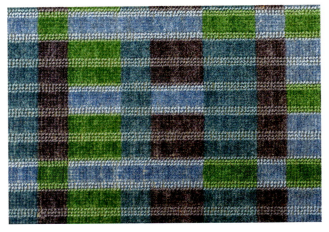

Above: Straub designed the instantly recognisable moquette pattern for the London Underground seat fabric

In 1953, Straub moved to the Essex village of Great Bardfield and became friends with artists John Aldridge, Edward Bawden, and Audrey Cruddas. Together they held "open house" exhibitions, attracting national press attention and luring thousands to visit the village during the summers of 1954, 1955, and 1958.

While Straub continued to work with Warner until 1970, she was also enlisted by British-based textile designer Isabel Tisdall to create designs for her newly launched company Tamesa Fabrics, which began trading in 1964. Her work stood out for its use of bold, bright colours in innovative combinations while at the same time using strong, durable, functional fabrics.

Most notably, Straub's designs for Tamesa were used on BEA's Trident passenger aircraft, and on the RMS *Queen Mary* and *Queen Elizabeth 2* ocean liners. Her blue/green moquette design was used on all London Transport buses and trains entering service from 1969 to 1978. These designs remained familiar to commuters and travellers for decades to come, into the early years of the Millennium.

Straub also became an influential textile teacher at a number of London colleges, including the Central School of Art & Design, the Hornsey College of Art, and the Royal College of Art. She spoke at the International Handicrafts Conference at Dartington Hall and advocated for the preservation of knowledge among the handicraft community.

On retirement in 1970, she left Great Bardfield and moved to Cambridge, but continued to be interested in cloth and weaving. She was made a Royal Designer for Industry in 1972, an honour given by the British Royal Society of Arts (RSA) to a select few. In 1977, she published the book *Hand Weaving and Cloth Design*.

To mark her 50th year as a designer, in 1984 the RSA held the first retrospective exhibition of her work, which travelled around the UK. The show included the Silverton fabric that the institution had used for the refurbishment of its Fellows' Library in 1960.

The Design Council also published a monograph on Straub, the first textile designer to be included in its series on eminent 20th-century British designers.

In 1993 Straub received the Sir Misha Black Medal, given to creatives to recognize their role in design education. She was also made a Fellow of the Society of Industrial Artists and Designers (SIAD) and was awarded an OBE for services to textile weaving.

For the last years of her life she returned to her Swiss homeland, where she died in 1994, aged 85.

In a letter to curator, academic, and author Mary Schoeser shortly before her death, Straub described her design process thus: "Whilst thinking of the new cloth, I think of its weight, its draping qualities, the handle; I see it in colours. The essence of the whole exercise is to place the cloth, in my imagination, into the situation in which it will be used."

Above: The Helmsley pattern, 1951, at The Whitworth Art Gallery, The University of Manchester

PAUL RAND

"THE GREATEST LIVING GRAPHIC DESIGNER"
Steve Jobs

AMERICAN
1914–1996

HIGHLIGHTS
Logos for IBM, UPS, Enron, ABC, NeXT

CHARACTERISTICS
Use of the Swiss Style, simplicity and clarity, type-focused approach

Opposite: IBM poster designed by Rand

People who are passionate about left-field, avant-garde, and distinctly European ideas don't always like to admit it, but it's often when such ideas blend with the commercial needs of American capitalism that inventive and game-changing design work is created. And one such example is the iconic logo designs of Paul Rand.

The art director and graphic designer was one of the first commercial artists in the US to embrace and practice the Swiss Style of graphic design. This movement, which emerged in Switzerland during the 1950s, expanded and formalized the Modernist typographic innovations that grew out of 1920s art movements such as Constructivism in Russia, De Stijl in the Netherlands and the Bauhaus in Germany.

Under the influence of this approach, Rand's corporate logo designs for IBM, UPS, Enron, Morningstar, Westinghouse, ABC, NeXT, and others have become iconic, and remain a huge influence on graphic designers across the world.

Rand was born Peretz Rosenbaum in 1914, in Brooklyn, New York. His design career began at an early age, painting signs for the family grocery store. However, his father didn't believe art would make a good career. Consequently, Rand was only able to study art in night classes and was largely self-taught, learning from imported European magazines. However, he later attended several art schools in succession, including the Parsons School of Design, the Art Students League, and Yale University in Connecticut.

Above: Paul Rand in front of one of his designs

His first job in the profession was a part-time position creating stock graphics for a syndicate that sold them to newspapers and magazines. In his work there, he drew influence from the German advertising style known as *Sachplakat* ("object poster") and the works of Danish industrial designer Gustav Jensen.

To contemporaries in his profession, this all might have sounded pretentious and overly "artsy." But in Rand's eyes it was the opposite. Under the influence of these masters, he believed that the purpose of graphic design was to use simplicity and geometry to become a universal language that everyone could understand.

With this in mind, it's no coincidence that around this time he decided to change his name for one that would sit more comfortably in corporate America. Aside from sounding less obviously Jewish, Paul Rand was also snappier and more symmetrical, with four letters in each name. In a way, it can be seen as the first corporate identity he created.

Rand's reputation in the profession grew when he began designing covers for Direction magazine. He did the work pro bono, on the condition that he would have full artistic freedom. His designs attracted praise from the likes of László Moholy-Nagy,

Above: Jazzways Cover of the one off jazz magazine from Cincinatti published in 1946

a Hungarian painter and photographer who was a professor in the Bauhaus school. "He is an idealist and a realist, using the language of the poet and businessman," Moholy-Nagy wrote. "He thinks in terms of need and function. He is able to analyze his problems, but his fantasy is boundless."

In the 1930s Rand's reputation grew as a result of his page layouts and cover designs, and he became art director of *Esquire* and *Apparel Arts* magazines. From 1941 to 1954 he worked as art director of the William H. Weintraub advertising agency, where he advocated ads in which words and pictures were integrated, working together rather than fighting each other.

To modern advertisers, that all may sound like standard practice. But it is only so because pioneers like Rand fought for this integrated approach, which eventually became mainstream. His ads for clients such as Ohrbach's department store also took a stripped-down approach to copywriting and design, making both more effective by making both simpler. This also translated to his logo designs for IBM, ABC, Cummins Engine, UPS, Enron, and others, which were minimalist and simple while still being inventive and eye-catching. Most of them have become icons of 20th-century design, and some are still in use.

Rand continued to design corporate identities into the eighties and nineties for a rumoured $100,000 per project. The most notable of his later works was his collaboration with Steve Jobs on the NeXT Computer corporate identity. While the computer is long forgotten, the logo remains a design classic.

Rand drew influences from multiple sources, and saw that as a strength. "The artist is a collector of things imaginary or real," he wrote. "He accumulates things with the same enthusiasm that a little boy stuffs his pockets. The scrap heap and the museum are embraced with equal curiosity. He takes snapshots, makes notes, and records impressions on tablecloths or newspapers, on backs of envelopes or matchbooks. Why one thing and not another is part of the mystery, but he is omnivorous."

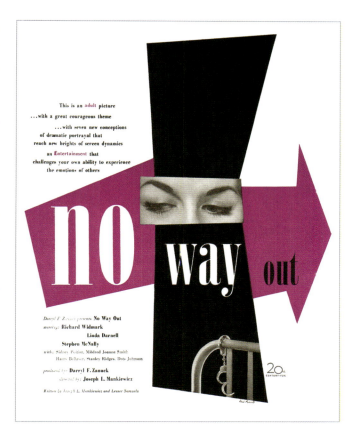

Above: 1950 US advertisement for the film No Way Out starring Richard Widmark, Linda Darnell and Stephen McNally

> *"DON'T TRY TO BE ORIGINAL, JUST TRY TO BE GOOD."*
>
> Paul Rand

In 1996 Rand died aged 82. Shortly before his death, Jobs described him as "the greatest living graphic designer." But good design isn't the only reason why Rand is revered by the profession. Perhaps his greatest contribution was convincing corporate America that design was not an optional extra, but essential for their bottom line.

In doing so, he spearheaded a revolution in which "commercial artists" became known as graphic designers, with the added respect and compensation that this enhanced position brought. As graphic designer Louis Danziger wrote in *Print* magazine in 1997, "Anyone designing in the 1950s and 1960s owed much to Rand, who largely made it possible for us to work. He, more than anyone else, made the profession reputable."

Above: Book Week poster 1958

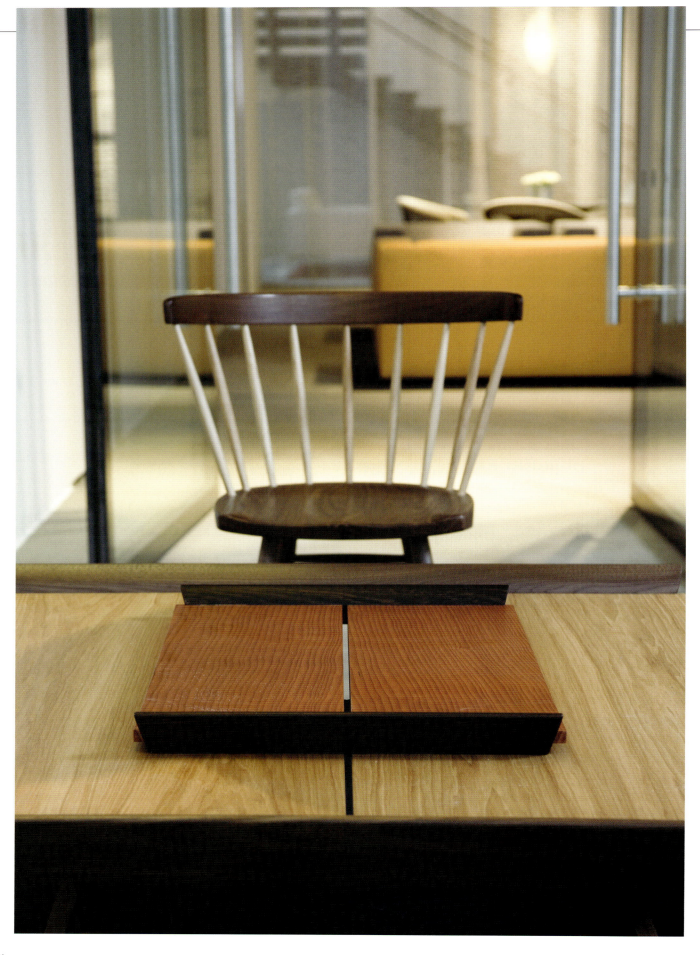

FLORENCE KNOLL

KNOWN AS AN ARCHITECT AND AN INTERIOR AND FURNITURE DESIGNER, FLORENCE KNOLL MOVED AMONG DISCIPLINES WITH EASE.

AMERICAN
1917–2019

HIGHLIGHTS
Interior design, furniture design

CHARACTERISTICS
Rationalized space, Modernist influences, natural materials

Opposite: Knoll showroom, London, UK

Above: Florence Knoll in her studio in 1961

Knoll is perhaps best known for bringing the principles of Modernist design into office interiors. Today, the best-designed offices typically feature open environments, clean lines, and geometric shapes – and for that we owe her a debt of gratitude.

She was born Florence Marguerite Schust in 1917, in Saginaw, Michigan. Her father, a superintendent of a commercial bakery, died when she was just five. Her mother died when she was 12, and Florence was placed under legal guardianship and sent to Kingswood School Cranbrook, a local boarding school for girls.

There, she was mentored by Kingswood art director Rachel de Wolfe Raseman, and together they designed a home that integrated interiors and exteriors, sparking a lifelong interest in architecture. Florence proceeded to spend a series of fruitful years in art education, albeit ones that were repeatedly interrupted by bouts of ill health.

The home project brought her to the attention of Eliel Saarinen, president of the Cranbrook Academy of Art. She went on to spend summers with his family in Finland and befriended his son, Eero, who gave her impromptu architectural history lessons. Florence went on to study architecture at Cranbrook for a year, 1934–35, then studied town planning at the School of Architecture at Columbia University.

In 1936–37 she explored furniture making with Eero Saarinen (who by then had become an architect and industrial designer) and designer, architect, and filmmaker Charles Eames (see Chapter 13). Then, in 1938–39, on the recommendation of Finnish architect and designer Alvar Aalto, she attended the Architectural Association in London, where she was influenced by Swiss-French architect Le Corbusier's International Style.

She left Britain just as war was breaking out and moved to Cambridge, Massachusetts, where she worked briefly as an unpaid apprentice for German-American architect Walter Gropius and Bauhaus architect and furniture designer Marcel Breuer (see Chapter 8). In 1940 she enrolled at the Chicago Armour Institute (now Illinois Institute of Technology), under the tutelage of German-American architect Ludwig Mies van der Rohe, and finished her BA in architecture in 1941.

She moved to New York, taking jobs with several architects, including Harrison & Abramovitz. There, she was assigned interiors on the basis of her gender, and worked with a German-American designer, Hans Knoll, to design an office for Republican politician Henry Stimson.

In 1943 Florence joined Hans Knoll's small furniture company and founded its interior-design service, the Knoll Planning Unit. The two married in 1946, and she became a full business partner of the company, Knoll Associates, Inc. Post-war, the US experienced an office building boom, and the Knoll Planning Unit took full advantage as it began offering innovative full-service design solutions for office interiors, including everything from space planning to furniture selection. Knoll also advanced the science of office design, not just decorating the space but analyzing the client's work requirements (which she determined through interviews) and designing functional spaces that would meet those needs.

Below: Knoll showrooms highlight the modern design aesthetic that Florence brought to interiors

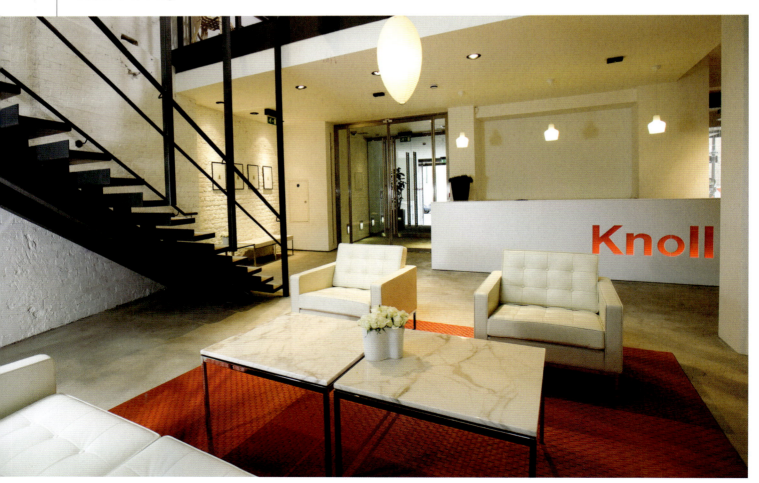

Central to their offering was the signature Knoll Look, marked by rationalized space plans, modern furniture, sleek geometries, and an integration of structure, colour, and texture. This contrasted heavily with the general approach to office decoration at the time, which was characterized by antique and period styles. For instance, the traditional heavy mahogany desk was replaced with light and sleek modern designs. Spaces were made to be more open, with seating areas for informal discussions. Conference tables were remade into a boat shape so that people could see one another more clearly.

The underlying philosophy to all this was what Knoll saw as a "total design" or "Bauhaus approach," where interior architecture, furniture, lighting, textiles, and art were integrated. Knoll also brought colour, texture, and organic shapes to interiors inspired by Modernism, making them more comfortable for everyday use. This "softer Modernism" was seen as more appealing to ordinary people.

When existing furniture didn't meet her needs, Knoll designed her own, including tables, desks, chairs, sofas, benches, and stools. They were characterized by sleek silhouettes and clear geometries, reflecting her architectural training and interests. And that was no accident; she believed the skills used to design buildings should translate to furniture. In that light, she also persuaded architects including Eero Saarinen, Marcel Breuer, Pierre Jeanneret, and Hans Bellmann to design furniture for Knoll.

The Unit completed over 70 office interiors, including those of IBM, GM, Look magazine, Seagram, Heinz, Connecticut General Life Insurance Company and CBS. It ran on a small team, typically eight designers and two drafters, although as the volume of projects dramatically increased, the staff grew to around 20. Knoll provided extensive education and mentoring to the designers who worked under her, and many Knoll Planning Unit designers went on to found interiors divisions at architectural firms such as SOM.

Above: Some more of the office furniture Knoll popularized

Above: One of Knoll's sleek bench designs

When Hans died in a car accident in 1955, Florence took over as president. In 1960 she moved to Florida with her second husband, Harry Hood Bassett, but stayed in charge of design at Knoll until 1965. In 2019 she died in Florida aged 101.

Unlike many female designers of the era, she was recognized in her lifetime, and received many awards and honours. In 1985 she was inducted into the Interior Design Hall of Fame, and in 2002 President George W. Bush presented her with the nation's highest award for artistic excellence, the National Medal of Arts. She was also awarded honorary doctorates from the universities of Vermont, Miami, and Minnesota.

Before Florence Knoll, interior design was mostly seen as a hobbyist pursuit that only applied to domestic spaces. By pioneering it as a professional discipline and applying it to office environments, she forever changed the way workplaces look. As New York Times architecture critic Paul Goldberger wrote, she "probably did more than any other single figure to create the modern, sleek, post-war American office, introducing contemporary furniture and a sense of open planning into the work environment."

LUCIENNE DAY

"DAY'S [DESIGNS] HAVE AN ENDURING FRESHNESS AND VERVE..."

Lesley Jackson

BRITISH
1917–2010

HIGHLIGHTS
Abstract pattern-making

CHARACTERISTICS
Bright colours, stylized florals, geometric shapes

Opposite: Calyx screen-printed curtain fabric for Heal Fabrics, 1951

One of the most influential British textile designers of the 1950s and 1960s, Lucienne Day drew on inspiration from other art disciplines to develop a new style of abstract pattern-making, now known as Contemporary Design.

She was born in Surrey, England, in 1917 and raised in Croydon by an English mother and a Belgian father who worked as a reinsurance broker. At 17 she enrolled at the Croydon School of Art, where she developed an interest in printed textiles. She went on to specialize in this discipline at the Royal College of Art in London from 1937 to 1940.

In her final year at RCA she met Robin Day, a furniture designer who shared her enthusiasm for modern design. They married in 1942 and set up their flat in Chelsea; it was decked out with her hand-printed textiles and his handmade furniture. However, wartime restrictions on textile manufacture meant that Day had to wait several years to begin her career as a designer, during which time she taught at Beckenham School of Art.

Above: Kyoto screen-printed curtain fabric for Cavendish Fabrics, 1975

Her first work in textiles came in the area of dress fabrics, where her clients included Stevenson & Sons and Cavendish Textiles. But she was keen to cross over into furnishings, and an important early client was Edinburgh Weavers, for which she designed two screen-printed furnishing fabrics in 1949 and woven furnishing fabric Martlet, 1945. The following year she was commissioned to design Fluellin, a stylized floral, by Heal's Wholesale and Exports (later known as Heal Fabrics). This marked the start of a long relationship with Heal's, which lasted until 1974.

The Festival of Britain in 1951 presented a great opportunity for Day to showcase her talents. She created textiles and wallpapers for the event, including her most famous design: Calyx, a furnishing fabric she created for an interior designed by her husband. Screen-printed on linen, Calyx was a large-scale abstract pattern composed of cup-shape motifs connected with spindly lines. The design was influenced by contemporary painters and sculptors such as Alexander Calder and Paul Klee.

Left: Lapis curtain fabric for Heal Fabrics, 1953

of Industrial Design, said in 1952, "These patterns are not stepping stones bridging the gulf between the historical and contemporary, nor halfway houses between the traditional and the experimental. They are boldly original and advanced."

In 1952, Day and her husband moved into a house at 49 Cheyne Walk in Chelsea. She transformed the interior into a model of Contemporary design, and the ground floor served as their joint studio for almost five decades. She also worked as a design consultant for John Lewis partnership during the 1970/80s and was made a Royal Designer for Industry (RDI) in 1962, an award established by the Royal Society of Arts.

Throughout the 1950s, Day's textiles were characterized by energetic rhythms and a spidery graphic style that might have looked spontaneous but demanded sophisticated technical skills to create, particularly their colourways and repeats. As well as purely abstract designs, she often created stylized organic patterns incorporating motifs such as skeletal leaves, spindly stems, feathery seed heads, and butterflies.

Toward the end of the decade she became influenced by new artistic trends such as Abstract Expressionism, and her designs for Heal's became more overtly painterly and larger in scale. During the 1960s she adopted brighter colours and simpler forms of expression, often featuring florals and geometric shapes including squares, circles, diamonds, and stripes. That said, she never abandoned her love of stylized florals and arboreal designs, which were recurrent motifs in her work.

Calyx sold in large quantities, leading Heal's to commission about six new furnishing fabrics every year that decade. It was a critical triumph too. Exhibited atthe Milan Trienniale in 1951, the fabric influenced a new generation of designers and inspired a whole new school of pattern-making, epitomizing the Contemporary style. The style was characterized by the replacement of floral motifswith non-representational patterns based on abstract art. Paul Reilly, chief information officer at the Council

Although Heal's was her principal client, Lucienne

LUCIENNE DAY

Right: Apex curtain fabric for Heal Fabrics, 1967

Day also designed for Liberty, British Celanese, John Lewis, and Thomas Somerset. Along with her fabrics, she created many celebrated designs in the fields of wallpaper and carpet.

Despite working in an era when women were expected to be full-time housewives and mothers, she was fully independent at work. And although she shared a studio with her husband, formal collaborations between the two were rare. One noteworthy exception were the interiors she designed for BOAC planes between 1961 and 1967. A second was their work as joint design consultants for John Lewis between 1962 and 1987, where they introduced a comprehensive house style affecting every aspect of the brand's design, from interiors to packaging.

In the mid-70s Lucienne withdrew from industrial

"[DAY'S DESIGNS]...ARE BOLDLY ORIGINAL AND ADVANCED."
Paul Reilly, Council of Industrial Design

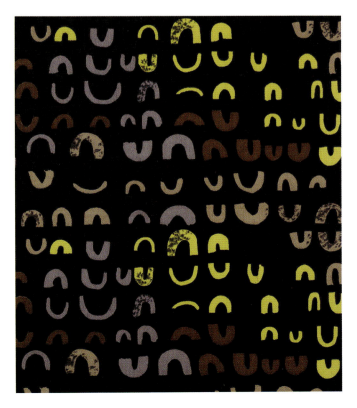

design to focus on purer forms of art and developed a whole new art form: one-off silk mosaic wall hangings. They were constructed from vibrantly coloured strips or squares of dyed silk, stitched together. Some featured abstract patterns while others sported stylized motifs, such as signs of the zodiac. Many were exhibited during the 1980s and 1990s at venues such as London's National Theatre and the Röhsska Museum in Gothenburg, Sweden.

In 2000 Day officially retired and began pursuing her interest in plants and her love of gardening. She died in 2010 aged 93. In her centenary year, 2017, design historian Lesley Jackson told *The Guardian* of Day's work's enduring appeal. "Whereas many other printed fabrics from the post-war period look rather quirky and mannered," she explained, "Day's have an enduring freshness and verve."

Left: Magnetic roller-printed curtain fabric for Heal Fabrics, 1957

SAUL BASS

"I SAW THE TITLE AS A WAY OF CONDITIONING THE AUDIENCE…"

AMERICAN
1920–1966

HIGHLIGHTS
Title sequences, film posters, corporate logos

CHARACTERISTICS
Kinetic typography to set mood, graphics-only movie posters

Opposite: The Man With The Golden Arm film poster

The opening title sequences for a movie do a lot of work in introducing the mood and theme of what viewers are about to see. And for that, we largely have Saul Bass to thank. He added movement to typography, revolutionizing a medium in which credits had previously been simply static title cards. For an encore, he went on to revolutionize movie posters too, as well as designing some of corporate America's most beloved logos.

Bass was born in 1920 in the Bronx, New York, to Eastern European Jewish immigrants. He drew constantly as a child, and in 1936 he received a fellowship to the Art Students League in Manhattan, where he studied under György Kepes, a Hungarian who was a master of the functional Bauhaus aesthetic. In 1938 Bass married Ruth Cooper and they went on to have two children.

After graduating, Bass freelanced as an advertising designer before moving to Los Angeles in 1946. In 1950 he joined Foote, Cone & Belding; two years later he started his own company. Bass mainly did mundane print work for film posters until he got his first big break collaborating with filmmaker Otto Preminger to design the movie poster for his 1954 film *Carmen Jones*. Preminger was so impressed, he asked him to design the title sequence as well.

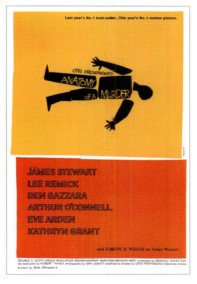

Above: Anatomy of a Murder poster

This was a crucial opportunity for Bass, whose innovation was to extend such sequences beyond the functional (a list of names) and use kinetic (i.e. moving) typography and synchronize it with the audio and other visuals to create a dramatic atmosphere. He said, "My initial thoughts about what a title can do was to set mood and the prime underlying core of the film's story, to express the story in some metaphorical way. I saw the title as a way of conditioning the audience, so that when the film actually began, viewers would already have an emotional resonance with it."

It was not until the following year, though, that people really started to notice Bass's work, when he designed the poster and title sequence for Preminger's *The Man with the Golden Arm* (1955).

Top: Storyboards for the Spartacus film titles

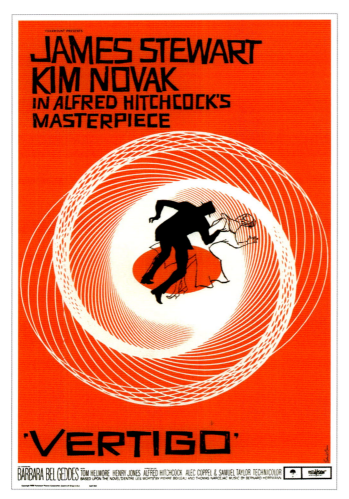

Above: Saul Bass's poster for the film Vertigo

Both featured the disembodied arm of an addict, with gold lettering nodding to "gold" as a slang term for heroin. Drug abuse was a taboo subject at the time, and the sequence was immediately controversial. Consequently, Bass was hired by Alfred Hitchcock, and he went on to develop a succession of iconic sequences for the director. Most memorably, the credits for *North by Northwest* (1959) race up and down what eventually becomes a high-angle shot of a skyscraper, while the opener for *Psycho* (1960) features disjointed text that races together and apart in manic fashion.

…THIS APPROACH OF USING KINETIC TYPOGRAPHY FOR TITLE SEQUENCES GRADUALLY BECAME THE NORM…

Title sequences created by Bass became part of the excitement of watching a movie. Film reels were delivered to cinemas with the instruction "Projectionist—pull curtain before titles." He continued to create title credits in this fashion, including for *Spartacus* (1960), *West Side Story* (1961), *It's a Mad, Mad, Mad, Mad World* (1963), *Big* (1988), *The War of the Roses* (1989), *Goodfellas* (1990), *Cape Fear* (1991), and *Casino* (1995). And this approach of using kinetic typography for title sequences to set an atmosphere gradually became the norm across the movie and TV landscapes.

This in itself would be enough to secure Bass a place in graphic-design history. But he's also famed for something else. Before Bass, movie posters typically featured the main actors or key scenes. For instance, for his first commission, *The Man with the Golden Arm*, one would have expected a poster featuring lead actor Frank Sinatra. Instead Bass's poster featured a jagged arm and abnormal typography. In doing so, he launched a signature style that used graphics instead of stars to portray the subject of the story and evoke an atmosphere.

It was an approach Bass used to great effect in posters that are still seen as classics. For instance, his poster for *Vertigo* (1958) featured abstract figures being sucked into a spiral vortex, capturing the anxiety and disorientation central to the film. Similarly, *Anatomy of a Murder* (1959) grabbed attention by featuring the silhouette of a corpse dissected into seven pieces.

These two classic designs, which remain popular art prints in homes and offices more than half a century on, exhibit many of the characteristics of Bass's poster style. Most obviously there's a minimalism and abstraction that reduces a theme or emotion down into its simplest form. There are also bold and expressive colours and masterfully precise typography. But there's also a fractured, splintered quality that points to a sense of unease, often reflecting the film's subject matter but also a more general fading of national confidence in a post-war, Cold War era.

This distinctive approach made Bass much in demand, and his posters for movies such as *The Magnificent Seven* (1960), *Birdman of Alcatraz* (1962), *Bunny Lake Is Missing* (1965), *The Two of Us* (1967), *The Human Factor* (1979), *The Shining* (1980), and *Return from the River Kwai* (1989) are seen as classics, even though not all of them were actually used by the movie studios at the time. He also created posters for film festivals; magazine, book and album covers; five Academy Award Presentation posters;

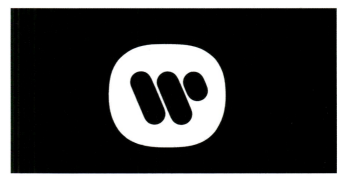

Above: Bass's design for Warner Communications logo

and the Student Academy Award for the Academy of Motion Picture Arts and Sciences.

Outside of the movies, Bass was responsible for some of the most iconic American logos of the 20th century. These include designs for Bell Telephone and its successor, AT&T; Continental Airlines; Dixie; United Airlines; Hanna-Barbera; Geffen Records; Girl Scouts of the USA; Kleenex; Quaker Oats; and Warner Communications. Logo design was a perfect fit for Bass's approach because it's all about graphically distilling an idea down to its most fundamental elements. In 2013, *Advertising Age* calculated that his logo designs had unusual longevity, averaging more than 34 years. Bass said, "The ideal trademark is one that is pushed to its utmost limits in terms of abstraction and ambiguity, yet is still readable. Trademarks are usually metaphors of one kind or another. And are, in a certain sense, thinking made visible."

Bass died in Los Angeles in 1996. Today, his moving-image collection of 2,700 items is held at the Academy Film Archive and is complemented by the Saul Bass papers at the Academy's Margaret Herrick Library. But his true legacy is not locked up in a museum; just turn on the TV and watch any modern movie, and you'll doubtless see his influence in the opening-credits sequence.

Below: The poster for Bunny Lake is Missing

MILTON GLASER

GRAPHIC DESIGNER, PAINTER, AND EDUCATOR, MILTON GLASER BROUGHT DESIGN TO EVERYDAY LIFE.

AMERICAN
1920–2020

HIGHLIGHTS
"I♥NY" logo, *New York* magazine, DC Comics logo, Bob Dylan's Greatest Hits poster

CHARACTERISTICS
Psychedelic graphics, silhouettes, geometric outlines

Opposite: The famous and much-copied Dylan Thomas poster by Milton Glaser

Milton Glaser is considered one of the most influential designers of the 20th century for two main reasons. First, he was co-founder of Push Pin Studios, an American design firm that helped shape the look of the 1960s; and second, because he designed the iconic "I♥NY" logo, one of the world's most recognizable symbols.

Glaser was born in 1929 in the Bronx, New York, to Hungarian Jewish immigrants. As a child, he remembers an older cousin drawing a bird on the side of a paper bag. "I almost fainted with the realization that you could create life with a pencil," he told *Inc.* magazine in 2014.

He attended the High School of Music and Art, then the Cooper Union School of Art, before earning a scholarship to study at the Accademia di Belle Arti (Academy of Fine Arts) in Bologna, Italy. In 1952, he co-founded a design agency in New York called Push Pin Studios with Reynold Ruffins, Seymour Chwast, and Edward Sorel.

The studio wasn't just a commercial enterprise but a principled one, driven by a philosophy that rejected tradition and favoured reinterpreting past styles in a fresh light—everything from wood-cut illustration and Victoriana to Art Deco, Art Nouveau, and comic books. Glaser and Chwast directed Push Pin Studios for 20 years, and it became hugely influential in the world of graphic design for its record sleeves, books, magazines, posters, corporate logotypes, and font design.

In 1968, Glaser established New York magazine in partnership with Clay Felker. The magazine became the inspiration for similar titles in cities around the world. Glaser remained art director and president until 1977. From 1975 to 1977 he was also vice-president and design director of *The Village Voice*.

In 1974 he launched his own design firm, Milton Glaser Inc., and left Push Pin Studios the following year. The company, which is still in business, produced print designs such as logos, brochures, annual reports, and signage, along with environmental and interior designs, for clients including Target, Eleven Madison Park, Brooklyn Brewery, and the Rubin Museum of Art.

Left: Brooklyn lager label design

Left: The DC Comics logo in different colours

Below: The worldwide recognisable logo that has become synonymous with New York City

In 1983 Glaser launched publication-design firm WBMG in partnership with Walter Bernard. The company designed more than 50 magazines, newspapers, and periodicals around the world and was responsible for the complete redesign of three major newspapers: *The Washington Post*, *La Vanguardia* in Barcelona, and *O Globo* in Rio de Janeiro.

Over the course of his career, Glaser personally designed and illustrated more than 400 posters in his signature style, which mixed inspiration from early-20th-century artists with psychedelic graphics, blasts of colour, silhouettes, and geometric outlines. One of his most celebrated posters was one of his first; it was a design for Bob Dylan's *Greatest Hits* in 1966, and was inspired by Art Nouveau and Marcel Duchamp's 1957 *Self-Portrait in Profile*. Other Glaser designs that remain instantly recognizable include the Brooklyn Brewery logo, the DC comics logo, and the AIDS logo for the World Health Organization. He designed several typefaces that are still in use, including Glaser Stencil, which drew inspiration from geometric sans-serif fonts such as Futura and Avant Garde.

His most celebrated design, however, has to be his "I♥NY" logo. It came at a pivotal time, 1977, when crime and violence were high and the city was on the verge of bankruptcy. When the State of New York hired Glaser and ad agency Wells Rich Greene to design a logo to increase tourism, the story goes that Glaser sketched the design while sitting in the back of a taxi on the way to the meeting.

"I'M FLABBERGASTED BY WHAT HAPPENED TO THIS LITTLE, SIMPLE NOTHING OF AN IDEA."

Milton Glaser

MILTON GLASER

The simple but instantly effective graphic was inspired by pop artist Robert Indiana's Love design, and was donated to the city. Today the logo appears on everything from coffee cups to T-shirts and hats, and is estimated to earn the state $30m a year. After the September 11 terrorist attacks, it became even more of a symbol of civic pride, and appeared on T-shirts and caps everywhere. "I'm flabbergasted by what happened to this little, simple nothing of an idea," Glaser told *The Village Voice* in 2011.

Aside from his own creations, Glaser was a tireless advocate for the importance of design. From 1961 onwards he served as a board member and instructor at the School of Visual Arts. He was also vice-president of the American Institute of Graphic Arts and The International Design Conference.

Above: Milton Glaser receiving the National Medal of Arts from President Barack Obama in 2009

Glaser continued working into his nineties. In 2004 he won a National Design Lifetime Achievement Award from Cooper Hewitt, Smithsonian Design Museum. In 2008 he was the subject of a documentary, *Milton Glaser: To Inform and Delight*. And in 2009 he was awarded the National Medal of Arts by President Barack Obama and First Lady Michelle Obama at the White House. He was the first graphic designer to receive the award.

However, this establishment acceptance didn't mean that Glaser ever mellowed. The war between art and commerce continued to bedevil him, and in 2019 he told *Computer Arts* magazine, "The key elements in my professional life that have had the most influence have been the alarming degree of control over all graphic projects by marketing and advertising companies. Every idea is dominated by previous historical success, which tends always to protect profitability by creating things that are already familiar. This is not a great environment for the imagination, in search of meaning."

Milton Glaser died in 2020, on his 91st birthday. The previous year, he had redesigned the historical "chino" logo of Italian communication agency Pomilio Blumm; a documentary based on the project, *A Social Design Story*, is available on streaming platforms.

Left: 1984 print advertisement for Perrier

JACQUELINE CASEY

"I LEARNED HOW A DESIGN COULD BE AT ONCE SWISS IN ITS CLEANNESS, ITALIAN IN ITS IMAGINATION, AND PLAYFUL LIKE JACKIE HERSELF."

Nicholas Negroponte

AMERICAN
1927–1992

HIGHLIGHTS
MIT posters and other designs

CHARACTERISTICS
Bold typography, striking images, use of Swiss Style, visual puns

Opposite: Promotional poster for an exhibition by James Turrell, held at Hayden Gallery, MIT, Cambridge, MA, 1983

Above right: Design for Robert Mapplethorpe's Lisa Lyon, 1982

Early in their careers, designers often have a dilemma on their hands. Working for an established institution provides stability and security but often limits the scope of creative possibilities. In contrast, working as a freelancer or setting up one's own business may be less stable, but can provide wider opportunities to create work future generations will remember.

Jacqueline Casey is a rare example of a designer who achieved both. She worked for one organization, the Massachusetts Institute of Technology (MIT), throughout her entire career. And yet rather than being limited creatively, she produced iconic work that influenced a generation and is still celebrated.

The only child of a working-class couple, she was born Jacqueline Shepard in 1927 in Quincy, Massachusetts. As a student, she earned a Bachelor of Fine Arts degree in fashion design and illustration at the Massachusetts College of Art, graduating in 1949. Afterwards she took a number of jobs, including work in interior design and advertising, but never settled in any of them; so she took a three-month trip around Europe to clear her head. She returned convinced that she wished to pursue a career in the visual arts.

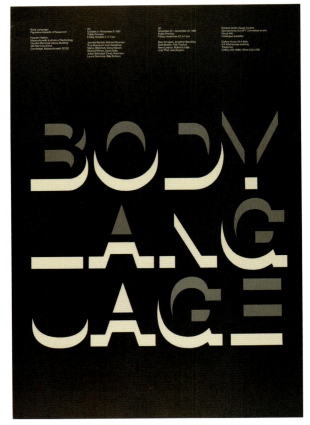

Left: Promotional poster for Connections

Above: Body Language: Figurative Aspects of Recent Art poster design

MIT is known for producing some of the world's leading scientists, engineers, and tech founders. But it was also the first American college to employ graphic designers, and Shepard was among that early intake. They were responsible for crafting the graphic design for the university's publishing arm—which later became known as MIT Press—as well as campus projects and other programs, and cultural and scientific events organized by the university.

> "THERE WAS AN OPPORTUNITY TO LEARN SOMETHING NEW EVERY DAY."
>
> Jacqueline Shepard

Shepard became a graphic designer in the Office of Publications (later the Office of Design Services) from 1955. She was hired by MIT's first design director, Muriel Cooper, a friend from art school. Aside from opportunities to be creative, Shepard relished learning at one of the nation's greatest universities. "In my early days at MIT, a designer working on summer materials would interview faculty and have a mini-course in a subject such as radioisotopes from the professor in charge," she recalled. "There was an opportunity to learn something new every day."

In 1958 Shepard married William Casey and changed her name to Jacqueline S. Casey. In 1972 she became director, and was one of few women working at this level at MIT at the time. During her tenure she became known for designing distinctive publicity posters for MIT events, working alongside Ralph Coburn and Dietmar Winkler.

JACQUELINE CASEY

Right: Poster for the concert Glorious is the Name of Jesus: A Celebration of Gospel Music, held at MIT, Cambridge, 1986

She was influenced by the International Typographic Style, aka Swiss Style, which had been developed in Switzerland by designers including Karl Gerstner, Armin Hofmann, and Josef Müller-Brockmann.

Casey's MIT posters typically consist of a striking image or bold typography accompanied by informational details in smaller text. She also characteristically used typographic wordplay and visual puns. She said, "My job is to stop anyone I can with an arresting or puzzling image, and entice the viewer to read the message in small type, and above all to attend the exhibition."

She was a guest lecturer at museums and schools including the Massachusetts College of Art, Yale University, Carnegie-Mellon University, Cooper Union, and Kent State, and a judge of several national exhibitions. Casey was also a member of the Alliance Graphique Internationale and the American Institute of Graphic Arts, and received numerous awards for her work.

Casey was diagnosed with cancer in 1982 and struggled to handle her MIT workload. In 1989 she was forced to retire, although she continued to work as a visiting scholar at the MIT Media Laboratory. She died of cancer in 1992 aged 65.

That same year, her book Posters: *Jacqueline S. Casey 30 Years of Design at MIT* was published. Joseph P. Ansell, chair of visual arts at Otterbein College in Ohio, wrote that Casey had created "some of the most elegant posters in America… Her sense of proportion is at once precise and measured, organic and humane. These seemingly opposite qualities are clearly appropriate for her subjects and her audience. Through careful analysis, Casey uncovers the essence of each subject and communicates the creative spark which is the source of all."

In that same book, Nicholas Negroponte, director of the MIT Media Lab, recalled how much he had learned from her. "I learned how a design could be at once Swiss in its cleanness, Italian in its imagination, and playful like Jackie herself," he wrote. "Jackie always says she cannot teach. Ha! She doesn't need to. She has already taught thousands of young designers through her work. Those of us who have had the privilege of working with Jackie did nothing but learn from her insights."

Today, the MIT Museum holds an archive of her complete works for the university, and mounted exhibitions in 1992, 2012, and 2018. Work is also held in the permanent collections of the Library of Congress, the Museum of Modern Art, and Cooper Hewitt, Smithsonian Design Museum. The Rochester Institute of Technology also has a collection of 99 posters donated by the MIT Museum at the designer's request.

Below: Promotional poster for an event celebrating the life of Harold E. "Doc" Edgerton, MIT, 1990

MAIJA ISOLA

ISOLA BROUGHT ENERGY AND INNOVATION TO THE WORLD OF TEXTILE DESIGN AND WAS PIVOTAL TO THE SUCCESS OF FINNISH DESIGN HOUSE MARIMEKKO.

FINNISH
1927–2001

HIGHLIGHTS
Unikko (Poppy), Lokki (Seagull), Kivet (Stones)

CHARACTERISTICS
Bold, colourful, crisp outlines, flat patterns, influence of nature

Below: Marimekko Melooni design, with its characteristic ovals

Maija Isola's bold, colourful prints, inspired by her peripatetic life and parallel career as a visual artist, were a defining feature of the 1960s fashion scene, and continue to be popular. More broadly, she was a trailblazing free spirit who acted as a beacon for a new generation of women wishing to succeed in art and design.

Isola was born in 1927 in Riihimäki, Finland. She was the youngest of three sisters. Her father was a farmer who was also known for writing the lyrics to a popular Finnish Christmas carol.

In 1945 she married commercial artist Georg Leander, and their daughter, Kristina, was born the following year. Later, Isola studied at the Central School of Industrial Arts in Helsinki. On a trip to Oslo, in 1948, she visited art galleries and encountered the work of Edvard Munch; this inspired her first famous print, Amphora.

After graduating in 1949, Isola's student work was spotted by entrepreneur Armi Ratia, who hired her to work for textile-printing company Printex. In 1951 Ratia founded Marimekko, and Isola became its principal textile designer, creating eight to 10 patterns every year.

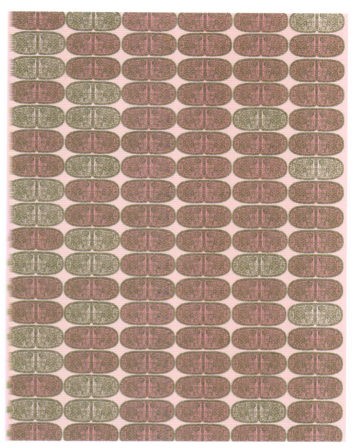

Above: Marimekko Tantsu Pink design

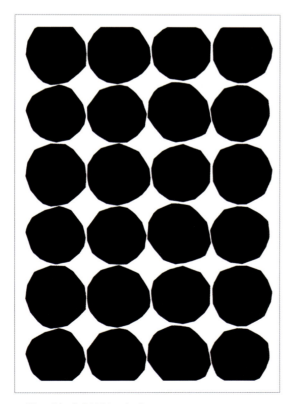

Above: Kivet Black & White design

Between 1957 and 1963 she created her first series of works on a single theme, Luonto (Nature). The series featured 30 designs based on pressed plants that her daughter Kristina had collected. In 1958 she began another series, Ornamentti (Ornament), based on Slavic folk art.

Isola's work was characterized by bold use of colour, crisp outlines, and flat patterning—an approach that echoed the growing Pop Art movement. They were hugely popular; post-war Europeans had endured enough drab misery and were crying out for some life and colour. Isola met that need by taking an innovative and groundbreaking approach to textile design.

She drew inspiration from nature, traditional folk art, modern visual art, and her travels in Europe, North Africa, and North America. She often worked in the evenings, sitting on the floor, and painted the original artwork across the entire width of a canvas. Sometimes she used real plants for her designs, and she composed the Kivet fabric, a print resembling giant stones, from circles cut out of coloured paper.

Above: The bold squiggles of the Lokki design

Outlining a typical scene, she wrote the following in a letter to her daughter in 1970: "I had a kind of huge floral still life spread out on the floor, wet, waiting to be rolled up... paints in yogurt pots, newspaper everywhere, and flowers in vases on the floor.... Big dark red roses, small fragrant and curiously hairy roses, yellow, orange and white poppies, water lilies in different shades of purple, black tulips and tiny carmine flowers whose names I don't know."

In her personal life, too, she was a free spirit, and her first two marriages did not last long. In 1959 she embarked on a third, marrying Jorma Tissari, a wealthy judge and art lover. When Isola felt that Marimekko was limiting her self-expression too much, her husband negotiated a new contract that gave her more creative freedom.

This was necessary, because their collaboration was often an adversarial one. Their most famous clash came when Isola defied Ratia's express dislike of floral patterns by painting the Unikko pattern in bold pink, red, and black on white. It became her, and Marimekko's, most famous creation.

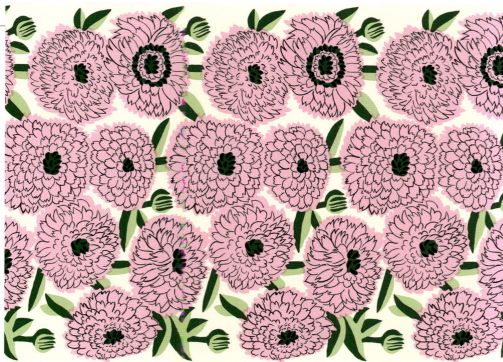

Left and Above: On the left, the era-defining Unikko pattern and above Primavera

The bold and eye-catching pattern was supremely versatile and radiated positive energy. It dovetailed nicely with the emerging "flower power" movement, in which protestors emphasized positive values such as peace and love. Most importantly, the design was a huge commercial success. Ultimately, it came to represent the Marimekko brand itself, and remains one of its most popular patterns.

From 1965 to 1967 Isola worked on the theme of sun and sea, creating at least nine designs that were adopted by Marimekko, including Albatrossi (Albatross), Meduusa (Jellyfish), and Osteri (Oyster). In 1970 she travelled to Paris to escape her marriage and family commitments, and began a relationship with Egyptian scholar Ahmed Al-Haggagi. He encouraged her to work on Arabian patterns, resulting in designs including Kuningatar, Naamio, Sadunkertoja, Tumma, and Välly. In 1971 the pair separated, and she spent three years in Algeria with a new lover named Muhamed.

In 1974 Isola designed the popular pattern Primavera, centred around stylized marigolds. In 1976 she returned to Paris, working with Al-Haggagi on another series of Egyptian-inspired prints including Niili (Nile), Nubia, and Papyrus. The following year, the two moved to North Carolina, in the US, where he was a lecturer. She made some designs there, but found it hard to sell any in America because few factories could print fabrics to her specifications.

In 1979 she returned to Finland, where she and Kristina designed patterns for Marimekko together until 1987. That year, Isola retired from her work in textiles to concentrate on her painting, which she pursued with great success until she died in 2001.

Isola's designs saw a resurgence in popularity in the 1990s and continue to be in demand today. More fundamentally, her work from the 1950s and 1960s is seen as iconic Finnish design and culture. Reflecting this fact, Finnair has been flying planes sporting a blue Unikko print since 2012. "Marimekko is close to our soul," the Finnish ambassador to the US, Ritva Koukku-Ronde, told *The Washington Post* in 2014. "The bright colours and the courageous designs all speak to our lifestyle."

"MARIMEKKO IS CLOSE TO OUR SOUL."

Ritva Koukku-Ronde, Finnish ambassador to the US

ADRIAN FRUTIGER

"...THE BEST GENERAL TYPEFACE EVER."

Erik Spiekermann

SWISS
1928–2015

HIGHLIGHTS
Univers, Frutiger, Avenir

CHARACTERISTICS
Legibility, elegance, universality

Opposite: Poster art using the Frutiger typeface

When we read anything—a book, newspaper, website, or signage—we take it for granted that the type will be easily readable. But that wouldn't be the case without the hard work of typeface designers and typographers. And one of the greatest 20th-century contributions to this field came from Swiss designer Adrian Frutiger.

With a passion for clarity and precision, Frutiger created some of the most popular typefaces of the 20th and 21st century including Avenir, Frutiger, Univers, and Vectora. He worked across three eras of type—hot metal, phototypesetting (the use of photography to make columns of type on photographic paper), and digital—and masterfully applied the same design principles in each of them. And if you've ever read a sign at an airport, bus station, or train station, you have a lot to thank him for.

Frutiger was born in 1928 in Unterseen, Switzerland, the son of a weaver. His interest in lettering began at an early age. As a boy he experimented with his own style of handwriting because he so disliked the

UNIVERS BECAME THE MODEL OF ALL HIS FUTURE TYPEFACES

formal cursive penmanship taught in Swiss schools. As a young man Frutiger landed an apprenticeship at the Otto Schlaefli printing house in Interlaken, and also took classes in woodcuts and drawing at the Gewerbeschule (trade school) in Bern, under Walter Zerbe, before landing work as a compositor at Gebr. Fretz in Zurich.

In 1949 he transferred to the Kunstgewerbeschule (School of Arts and Crafts) in Zurich, where he studied under Walter Käch, Karl Schmid, and Alfred Willimann until 1951. During this time Frutiger was mainly focused on calligraphy, but he also began sketching what would become the typeface Univers. After graduation he was recruited by Charles Peignot of Paris type foundry Deberny & Peignot.

Frutiger married his first wife in 1952, but she died two years later after the birth of their son. In 1955 he married theologian Simone Bickel, with whom he had two daughters. Sadly, both daughters experienced mental-health problems and committed suicide as teenagers. In response, he and his wife founded the Adrian and Simone Frutiger Foundation to fund psychology and neuroscience research and developments in mental-health support.

Frutiger's first commercial typeface was Président, a set of titling capital letters with small, bracketed serifs, released in 1954. This was followed by Ondine, a calligraphic, informal script typeface. The following year came Méridien, a glyphic, old-style serif text face with features that came to be seen as distinctively Frutiger—for example, an "a" in which the loop makes a horizontal line at the top on meeting the vertical.

In 1956 he designed the first of his most famous and popular typefaces: Univers. A neo-grotesque sans-serif based on Akzidenz-Grotesk, it was marketed with a

"THE QUALITY OF THE DRAFTSMANSHIP—RATHER THAN THE INTELLECTUAL IDEA BEHIND IT—IS MY MASTERPIECE."

design inspired by the periodic table. It was an instant hit, and Frutiger said it became the model for all his future typefaces.

In 1960 Frutiger established a design studio with André Gürtler and Bruno Pfäffli. Their commissions included logotypes, signage systems, and maps for clients such as Air France, IBM, and the Swiss Post Office. In 1964 Monotype commissioned him to create Apollo, its first typeface created specifically for phototypesetting.

In 1970 Frutiger was asked to design signage for the new Charles de Gaulle Airport in Paris. This new typeface needed to be legible both from afar and from an angle; Frutiger called it Roissy. Four years later, the Mergenthaler Linotype Company commissioned Frutiger to develop a print version of Roissy with improvements such as better spacing. It was released for public use under the name Frutiger in 1976.

Frutiger is essentially a mix of Univers tempered with organic influences of Gill Sans, a humanist sans-serif typeface by Eric Gill; Edward Johnston's type for London Transport; and Roger Excoffon's Antique Olive. Legible both from a distance and in small point sizes, it was hugely influential on the development of future humanist sans-serifs. Font designer Erik Spiekermann (see chapter 32) described it as "the best general typeface ever."

The 1970s saw a number of other major signage projects, including an adaptation of Univers for the Paris Métro and a slab-serif font for the Centre Pompidou. Then, in 1988, Frutiger completed another of his most famous creations, Avenir ("future" in French). His aim was to create a more human version of geometric sans-serifs popular in the 1930s, such as Erbar and Futura. He described it as his finest work, stating, "The quality of the draftsmanship—rather than the intellectual idea behind it—is my masterpiece."

Left: Adrian Frutiger at work in his studio in Bern, Switzerland

Other noteworthy typefaces designed by Frutiger include Centennial, Egyptienne, Glyphia, Iridium, Icone, OCR-B, Seifa, and Versailles as well as custom designs for corporations such as BP and Shiseido. He wrote several books about typography, including *Signs and Symbols; The Development of Western Type Carved in Wood Plates*; and *Geometry of Feelings*. He also taught for 10 years at the École Estienne, and for eight years at the École Nationale Supérieure des Arts Décoratifs, both in Paris.

Typeface design wasn't his only interest, however. In 2003, Swiss watchmaker Ventura commissioned him to design a watch face for a limited-edition line of wristwatches. He also designed three stamps for the Swiss Post Office to celebrate Swiss graphic design, and a wordmark for the National Institute of Design in Ahmedabad, India.

Frutiger continued working until late in his life. He collaborated with Heidrun Osterer and Philipp Stamm on an extensive autobiography, *Typefaces: The Complete Works*, which was published in 2008. The following year he partnered with Akira Kobayashi on a revised version of Frutiger: Neue Frutiger.

Frutiger died on 10 September 2015 at the age of 87. To this day, millions continue to benefit from his work on the legibility of signage (both directly and due to his influence on the profession as a whole). As Spiekermann wrote, "Frutiger is basically the best signage type in the world because there's not too much 'noise' in it, so it does not call attention to itself. It makes itself invisible, but physically it's actually incredibly legible."

KENJI EKUAN

"THE EXISTENCE OF TANGIBLE THINGS IS IMPORTANT. IT'S EVIDENCE THAT WE'RE HERE AS HUMAN BEINGS."
Kenji Ekuan

When at its best, design is about improving the lives of ordinary people. And in this regard there are few who can compare to Kenji Ekuan, one of Asia's greatest designers.

He was born in Tokyo in 1929 but spent his youth in Hawaii. At the end of the Second World War, he moved to Hiroshima, where he witnessed the atomic bombing of the city. After his father, a Buddhist monk, died from radiation poisoning, Ekuan joined Hiroshima temple, to succeed him. But he eventually changed course to become a designer; he said that the devastation caused by the bomb motivated him to become a "creator of things."

"Faced with brutal nothingness, I felt a great nostalgia for something to touch, something to look at," he told Japan's national broadcaster, NHK. "The existence of tangible things is important. It's evidence that we're here as human beings."

He went to study at Tokyo National University of Fine Arts and Music (now Tokyo University of the Arts) and graduated in 1955. Two years later, he founded GK Industrial Design Laboratory with some of his fellow graduates. GK stood for "Group of Koike;" Koike was the name of an associate professor at the university.

The company was the first in Japan to employ design specialists who would be commissioned by clients to design products; previously this role was only carried out within companies. Its slogans were "Democratization of Beauty" and "Democratization of Objects."

Ekuan's most famous creation was his soy sauce bottle for Kikkoman. Designed in 1961, the red-topped design is as iconic, ubiquitous, and recognizable in Japan as the Coca-Cola bottle is in America. Koike said he wanted to design a small, leakproof bottle because of his childhood memory of his mother pouring soy sauce from a big half-gallon container into a tabletop dispenser.

Other renowned works include the Komachi bullet train connecting Tokyo and northern Japan, and his chair designs for Japan Airlines, which won recognition from the Raymond Loewy Foundation. He also created logos for the Tokyo Metropolitan Government, Ministop convenience stores, and the Japan Racing Association.

JAPANESE
1929–2015

HIGHLIGHTS
1962 Kikkoman soy sauce bottle, Komachi bullet train, Narita Express

CHARACTERISTICS
Democratic, people-focused

Above: The shapely Kikkoman soy sauce bottle

Left: The nose of the Komachi bullet train

Below: The front of the Narita Express Train in Japan

KENJI EKUAN

"THE MOTORCYCLE IS SEX."
Kenji Ekuan

Right: Yamaha VMAX motorcycle

In 1989, GK Design Group formed an offshoot solely for vehicle design. GK Dynamics contracted with Toyota and Yamaha; the latter relationship lasted until 2014. Ekuan is celebrated for his 2008 redesign of the Yamaha VMAX motorcycle (which GK had first designed in 1995) as well as his quote, "The motorcycle is sex."

Ekuan was also involved in GK's design of the Narita Express, a popular train used to transport passengers between central Tokyo and Narita International Airport in Chiba. Its design won the 1992 Laurel Prize, an award specifically for railway vehicles.

Despite these big-ticket projects, though, Ekuan remained focused on designing small everyday items. As he told the Japan Times in 2001, "Design to me has always meant making people happy. Happy in the sense of creating items that provide comfort, convenience, function, aesthetics and ethics. I used to do a lot of research, fieldwork, wanting to understand the psychology of human needs and response."

More broadly, Ekuan worked to popularize Dougu theory, which views all things in the world, from everyday items to urban spaces, as tools. Essentially it sees things that people need, which are created by their will, as the "alter ego of their hands and feet" and the incarnation of their desires.

In the 1960s Ekuan participated in an architectural design movement called the Metabolism Movement, along with Masato Otaka, Fumihiko Maki, Kiyonori Kikutake, Kisho Kurokawa, Noboru Kawazoe, Kiyoshi Awazu, and others. And from the standpoint of industrial design, he promoted Dougu theory research, which explored new forms of living space using tools as a starting point.

He expressed his philosophy of design in his 1998 book *The Aesthetics of the Japanese* Lunchbox. His treatise examines how the bento box is a metaphor for the Japanese archipelago and a key to understanding the country's civilization.

In 1970 Ekuan became president of the Japan Industrial Design Association. Five years later he was elected president of the International Council of Societies of Industrial Design. He also served as chair of the Japan Institute of Design, dean of Shizuoka University of Art and Culture and a trustee of the ArtCenter College of Design.

Ekuan died in Tokyo in 2015 at the age of 85. Just a year previously, he had been given the Golden Compass Award in Italy, one of one of the world's highest accolades for an industrial designer and one of several international awards he accepted over the course of his career.

Above all, his work epitomizes a deep understanding of what design is and why it should be valued by society. "Regardless of what the object of design is, humans need design," he wrote. "For anything humans use in their day-to-day life, they need design and it is a clear and concrete proof of the fundamental human right to live."

MASSIMO VIGNELLI

"IF YOU CAN DESIGN ONE THING, YOU CAN DESIGN EVERYTHING."

ITALIAN
1931–2014

HIGHLIGHTS
American Airlines logo, New York City Subway map, *The Vignelli Canon*

CHARACTERISTICS
Modernist influences, use of geometric shapes

Opposite: Examples of the stacking Max cups and saucers

There are many types of designers featured in this book: product designers, textile designers, graphic designers, automobile designers and more. And it might seem, to the uninitiated, that some of them have little in common.

Massimo Vignelli's motto, however, was "If you can design one thing, you can design everything." And he put that principle into action in a career that spanned countless categories including packaging, houseware, furniture, public signage, and showroom design.

Vignelli was born in Milan in 1931. He was a classmate of graphic designer Heinz Waibl from 1946 to 1950 at the Arts High School in Milan, and of photographer Marirosa Toscani Ballo at the Brera Academy of Arts from 1948 to 1950. Vignelli then went on to study architecture at Milan Polytechnic (1951–1953) and the School of Architecture at the University of Venice.

Starting at the age of 16, he took a series of short internships with some of the best Italian architects and designers of the time, including Achille and Pier Giacomo Castiglioni, Giulio Minoletti, Giancarlo De Carlo, Franco Albini, and Ignazio Gardella. While in Venice, he designed lighting fixtures for his friend Paolo Venini—founder of the eponymous blown-glass company—including the iconic Fungo lamp in 1955.

In 1957 Vignelli married architect Elena Valle (who became Lella Vignelli) and the couple left for the US, where he was offered a fellowship at a silverware manufacturing company based in Newburyport, Massachusetts. At the same time, Lella started working at SOM, one of America's best-known architectural firms.

In 1960 they came back to Milan and opened the Massimo and Lella Vignelli Office of Design and Architecture, focusing on furniture, product, and graphic design. Their clients included Olivetti, Penguin Books, Piccolo Teatro, Pirelli, Poltronova, the Venice Biennial, and Xerox.

Then, in 1966, the couple moved to New York and Vignelli became one of the founders of Unimark, which is considered the first international design consultancy. He was design director and senior vice-president, coordinating the work of all its global offices and ensuring it was visually consistent. Lella, meanwhile, served as the head of interior design.

Vignelli's designs were famous for their minimal aesthetic and limited number of typefaces, including Akzidenz-Grotesk, Bodoni, Helvetica, Garamond No. 3, and Century Expanded. He himself described his approach to design as "semantically correct, syntactically consistent, and pragmatically understandable."

At Unimark, Vignelli created two of his best-known designs. The first was the American Airlines 1967 logo, although in truth Vignelli only designed half of what was released to the public. Vignelli's design was simply two A's in the Helvetica typeface—one red and one blue.

The airline insisted on the inclusion of the eagle, a symbol of the company. Vignelli refused, and the airline eventually had the office of Henry Dreyfuss add it to Vignelli's purely typographical design.

Another iconic creation was Vignelli's signage and map for the New York City Subway. Before then, the public-transport system in the city was an unholy mess of confusing and inconsistent signage, and uncoordinated, spaghetti-like maps. An influx of 52 million visitors for the 1964 New York World's Fair put a spotlight on these shortcomings.

Above: Vignelli's signage and map for the New York City subway

Taking his cue from Harry Beck's London Underground map (see Chapter 7), Vignelli sacrificed geographic precision in favour of geometric simplicity, and jettisoned any detail that wasn't strictly necessary for communicating how to get from A to B. The result was a colour-coded grid system with equally spaced stations that anyone could follow. Again, though, while considered a design classic, Vignelli's map was never distributed to the public. To the designer's annoyance, it was redesigned by the public authority several times before actually being printed.

In 1971 Vignelli left Unimark to establish his and his wife's own firm, Vignelli Associates, which opened offices in New York, Paris, and Milan. Their clients included IBM, Knoll, Bloomingdale's, the US National Park Service, Sotheby's, and American Airlines.

Soon Vignelli's creations were everywhere. Graphic designer Michael Bierut—a former employee at Vignelli Associates who has been a partner at Pentagram since 1990—wrote in 1981, "It seemed to me that the whole city of New York was a permanent Vignelli exhibition.

MASSIMO VIGNELLI

Left: Vignelli Center for Design Studies, Rochester Institute of Technology

Below: Study for Homage to the Square: with Saffron, Josef Albers, 1962

To get to the office, I rode in a subway with Vignelli-designed signage, shared the sidewalk with people holding Vignelli-designed Bloomingdale's shopping bags, walked by St. Peter's Church with its Vignelli-designed pipe organ visible through the window. At Vignelli Associates, at 23 years old, I felt I was at the center of the universe."

Vignelli was passionate about his profession and loved to share it with others. During his career, he taught at the Institute of Design at the Illinois Institute of Technology in Chicago, the Umanitaria School in Milan, the University of Venice School of Design, the Columbia University School of Architecture, the Philadelphia College of Art, and Parsons School of Design. He also gave lectures and workshops across China, Europe, and the United States. In 2009, he released a manual for young designers, *The Vignelli Canon* (now available as a free e-book).

He was a member of ADI, the Italian Association for Industrial Design, from its founding in 1956 and served on its board of directors from 1960 to 1964. He was also president of the Alliance Graphique Internationale from 1985 to 1988 and the American Institute of Graphic Arts from 1976 to 1977. He received multiple recognitions and awards, including lifetime achievement awards from the Brooklyn Museum and Cooper Hewitt, Smithsonian Design Museum.

In 2008, Vignelli and his wife agreed to donate the entire archive of their design work to the Rochester Institute of Technology. The archive was housed in a new building designed by the couple, which opened in September 2010 and features exhibition spaces, classrooms, and offices.

Vignelli died in 2014 in New York, aged 83, after a long illness. But his designs live on, as does the philosophy that inspired them.

In today's ever-changing world, designers increasingly need to be multi-disciplinary, and are often asked to design for technologies that are barely invented. In that light, one Vignelli teaching in particular stands out: "The discipline of Design is one, and can be applied to many different subjects, regardless of style," he wrote. "Very often people think that Design is a particular style. Nothing could be more wrong! Design is a discipline, a creative process with its own rules, controlling the consistency of its output toward its objective in the most direct and expressive way."

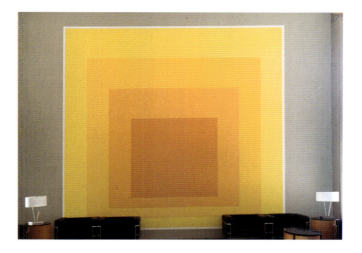

TERENCE CONRAN

"…WE COULD USE INTELLIGENT DESIGN TO CHANGE AND IMPROVE BRITAIN…"

BRITISH
1931–2020

HIGHLIGHTS
Furniture design, home decor

CHARACTERISTICS
Colourful, artful, affordable design with Bauhaus and Scandinavian influences

Opposite: Das Triest Hotel, Vienna, Austria

It's difficult for anyone under retirement age to imagine how grey, dull, and miserable life in post-war Britain was for ordinary people. The war had caused widespread destruction, and there was a shortage of food, housing, and other necessities. Many people were grieving the loss of loved ones. Rationing didn't fully end until 1954, almost a decade after the war ended.

In this light, what became known as the Swinging Sixties wasn't specifically about music, fashion, or art. It was fundamentally about a society where ordinary people were allowing themselves to feel good about life, and Britain's place in the world, for the first time in a generation. And helping them bring that fresh sense of colour, energy, and optimism into their homes, via stylish housewares and décor, was Terence Conran.

Conran was born in Kingston upon Thames, the son of Christina and Rupert, a South African-born businessman who owned a rubber importation company in East London. As a child, his mother encouraged him to express himself and provided him with the means to do so; his favourite present was a bag of wooden offcuts and a box of tools. He had an entrepreneurial spirit from an early age, and remembers exchanging a wooden battleship he'd made for a potter's lathe.

After attending schools in Hampshire and Dorset, Conran studied textiles and other materials at the Central School of Art and Design (now Central Saint Martins). While still a student, he established a furniture studio, sharing the space with one of his professors, Scottish artist Eduardo Paolozzi, one of the pioneers of the Pop Art movement.

In 1950 Conran left college to work for architect Dennis Lennon, and assisted in planning structures for the 1951 Festival of Britain. The following year he opened a furniture workshop, Conran & Company, in London's Notting Hill.

Above: The Conran Shop, London, UK

Conran went on to open a French-inspired restaurant in 1953. That same year, he had taken a trip to France with photographer Michael Wickham; it was the first time he'd been abroad, and it was a turning point in his life. "Coming from a very grey, post-war London I was amazed by the quality of everyday French life," he recalled in a Q&A with the Design Museum. "The delicious food in roadside cafés that was washed down with carafes of rough red wine, generously thrown in for free, and the simple, unpretentious but abundant displays on market stalls and shops. I thought, Why couldn't we enjoy a life like that back in England?"

He went on to open a coffee shop on London's King's Road in 1954. And then, in 1956, he formed the Conran Design Group, which incorporated his furniture company as well as furniture and interiors for homes, hotels, and restaurants. One of its most influential commissions was fashion designer Mary Quant's second Bazaar boutique, in Knightsbridge. Influenced by Italian designers Gio Ponti and Piero Fornasetti, Conran's design gave an informal, continental feel to the store.

Inspired by the Bauhaus and William Morris, Conran believed passionately that good design could improve the quality of everyday life, that it should be accessible to ordinary people, and that every designer should have a personal understanding of materials and processes. But in practice he soon discovered this alone wasn't enough.

"When I designed my first range of flat-pack furniture, Summa, we sold it to 80 retailers," he told *Elle Decor* in 2012. "But when I went to visit them and see how it was selling, I came back depressed. Not one retailer knew how to display it or understood the environment that went with it." This prompted Conran to open his own store, Habitat, in 1964. It quickly grew into a successful chain across the UK, and later expanded internationally, with the first store opening in Paris in 1973.

TERENCE CONRAN

Habitat wasn't just a commercial success; it was a cultural phenomenon. Its use of flat packaging, decades before the arrival of IKEA, was revolutionary in Britain at the time. Crucially, this approach allowed ordinary working people to afford artful, high-quality furniture, which had previously been the preserve of the wealthy. Habitat's furnishings and home goods were typically elegant and colourful as well as practical and affordable. The name Conran became virtually synonymous with good design.

A serial entrepreneur, Conran never stayed still for long. In 1980, with Fred Roche, he established the architecture and planning consultancy Conran Roche, which worked on projects in Europe, North America, and Asia. He opened other retail companies too, including the Conran Shop and Benchmark Furniture, and a series of restaurants. In 2005, he was named the most influential restaurateur in the UK by CatererSearch.

Conran was a highly driven and often difficult man who went through four marriages. He was occasionally guilty of self-mythologizing, and his business affairs were often tumultuous. But underpinning it all was a passion for design as a tool to improve people's lives.

Above: A wall mural at the Design Museum, London

Below: Terence Conran attends a press view at The Design Museum London, England, 2011

"COMING FROM A VERY GREY, POST-WAR LONDON I WAS AMAZED BY THE QUALITY OF EVERYDAY FRENCH LIFE."

Terence Conran

It was a philosophy that led him in 1989 to found the Design Museum in London, which he saw as his life's greatest achievement. "I'd been involved in selling design to the public and to industry for nearly 30 years, but I had a fierce conviction that we could do more," he wrote. "It was the feeling that we could use intelligent design to change and improve Britain, so acting as a catalyst for social and economic change."

Sir Terence Conran died on 12 September 2020 at the age of 88. In announcing the news, his family statement read, "He was a visionary who enjoyed an extraordinary life and career that revolutionized the way we live in Britain ... at the heart of everything he did was the very simple belief that good design improves the quality of people's lives."

DIETER RAMS

"LESS IS BETTER."

You've probably heard the phrase "less is more." But the motto Dieter Rams was famous for was "less is better." It's a subtle change to the phrase, but an important one. It informed a design philosophy that has led to many of the seminal domestic products of the 20th century, and more broadly influenced design, aesthetics, and culture.

As documentary director Gary Hustwit put it, "His work has influenced the way most of today's consumer products look and function. [When you read something on a computer or phone, it] looks the way it does because of Dieter Rams. Dieter's influence also extends to [his book *Ten Principles for Good Design*], a list of edicts that champions simplicity, honesty, and restraint, and still applies to design theory and practice today."

Rams was born in 1932 in Wiesbaden, Germany. As a child, he was strongly influenced by his grandfather, a carpenter. In 1947, he began his studies in architecture and interior decoration at the Handwerker- und Kunstgewerbeschule (School of Arts and Crafts), now part of the RheinMain University of Applied Sciences. A year later, he took a break to finish his carpentry apprenticeship, then returned in 1948 and graduated in architecture with honours in 1953.

His first job after graduation was for the Frankfurt-based architect Otto Apel. Then, in 1955, he landed a position with German consumer products company

GERMAN
B. 1932

HIGHLIGHTS
Electronic product design, furniture design, "less is better" philosophy, *Ten Principles for Good Design*

CHARACTERISTICS
Simplicity, functionality, minimalist aesthetics, durability

Above: The SK4 Radiogram

Above: A model poses with the Braun Transistor 1 Radio

Braun as an architect and interior designer. He was recruited by Erwin and Artur Braun following the death of their father, and his job was to modernize the company's interiors.

Rams became a protégé of Ulm School of Design luminaries Hans Gugelot, Fritz Eichler, and Otl Aicher, and quickly became involved in product design. In 1961 Rams became head of design at Braun, a position he retained for 36 years.

Rams made Braun a household name in the 1950s by designing electronic gadgets that were austere in their aesthetic yet user-friendly in their functionality. These included the famous SK 4 radiogram—known as "Snow White's coffin"—which was considered revolutionary for shifting household appliance design away from looking like traditional furniture. Other iconic devices from this era included the Braun SK 61 radiogram, the Braun Transistor 1 radio, the Braun TP 1 portable transistor radio and phonograph, and the Braun LE 1 speaker.

In 1959 Rams began a collaboration with Vitsœ+Zapf (now Vitsœ), leading to the development of the 606 Universal Shelving System, which is still sold today. He also designed furniture for UK furniture manufacturer Vitsœ in the 1960s, including the Vitsœ Model 601 lounge chair and the 620 chair collection.

The list of iconic designs he produced over the course of his career is endless. They include The Braun Lectron System, designed with Jürgen Greubel, a modular magnetic brick system designed as an educational aid in schools; the ET66 calculator, developed in collaboration with Dietrich Lubs; the Braun Dymatic pocket lighter, with its slim profile and functional aesthetic; the portable T1000 World Receiver; and the T3, T4, and T41 pocket radios. His approach to design and aesthetics was a big influence on Apple designer Jony Ive (see Chapter 46), and a number of Apple products pay direct tribute to Rams's work for Braun.

In the 1970s, Rams wrote his celebrated *Ten Principles for Good Design*, which became an essential part of the curriculum for design students. The principles are:

1 — Good design is innovative
2 — Good design makes a product useful
3 — Good design is aesthetic
4 — Good design makes a product understandable
5 — Good design is unobtrusive
6 — Good design is honest
7 — Good design is long-lasting
8 — Good design is thorough down to the last detail
9 — Good design is environmentally friendly
10 — Good design is as little design as possible

On the need to be environmentally sustainable, Rams was years ahead of most of the profession. In 1976 he delivered a prescient speech in New York in which he drew attention to an "increasing and irreversible shortage of natural resources," and called on designers to take more responsibility for the state of the world. He practised what he preached, too. Rams's designs were built to last for many years, typically by using high-quality materials and construction techniques that maximized long-term durability.

Above: Braun T41 Pocket Radio

Right: Braun Mach 2 lighter, designed by Dieter Rams and Florian Seiffert

DIETER RAMS

Above: The elegant simplicity of Braun calculators

"I imagine our current situation will cause future generations to shudder at the thoughtlessness in the way in which we today fill our homes, our cities and our landscape with a chaos of assorted junk," he said. In 1995 Rams published *Less But Better*, a book exploring some of the main products he produced at Braun and outlining his design philosophy of reducing waste, excess, and visual pollution, and living only with what is necessary.

Rams retired from Braun in 1997 but continues to work with Vitsœ. At the time of writing, Rams had been involved in design for seven decades and received a succession of honours and awards. He was the subject of a 2018 documentary, *Rams*, directed by Hustwit, and his work has been featured in numerous exhibitions. In reviewing a retrospective of his work at the Design Museum in 2009, *The Guardian* called him "the man who all but invented consumer product design as we know it today."

> "I IMAGINE OUR CURRENT SITUATION WILL CAUSE FUTURE GENERATIONS TO SHUDDER AT THE THOUGHTLESSNESS IN THE WAY IN WHICH WE TODAY FILL OUR HOMES."
>
> Dieter Rams

MARGARET CALVERT

HER ROAD SIGNS ARE INSTANTLY RECOGNIZABLE AND ARE CHARACTERIZED BY THEIR IMPRESSIVE CLARITY.

BRITISH
B. 1936

HIGHLIGHTS
Typography and icons for road and rail signage

CHARACTERISTICS
Use of mixed case, high-contrast colours, sans-serif typefaces

Opposite: The UK road sign indicating that wild animals may come into the road

Britain has one of the best road-safety records in the world despite being a densely packed island with a complex road network. The unsung heroes at the heart of this success are clear, well-defined, and instantly recognizable road signs. And so the UK owes a large debt to the pioneering work of typographer and graphic designer Margaret Calvert.

She was born in South Africa in 1936 and moved to England in 1950, aged 14. She studied at the Chelsea College of Art, where she specialized in illustration and printmaking. There, she became interested in commercial art under the mentorship of graphic artist Jock Kinneir.

Just as she was sitting her finals, Kinneir gave Calvert her first job: helping design the signage for Gatwick Airport. In 1957 they created a sophisticated design system with an accompanying brand manual that explained it. For clarity and consistency, they ensured all signs were designed with the same colour system (black on yellow) and standardized typography with thick lines and heavy icons that were recognizable at a distance. Their work was highly acclaimed and had a big influence on signage design across the airline industry.

Shortly afterwards, P&O asked Kinneir and Calvert to create a colourful luggage-labelling system for its freight ships. While Kinneir created the main labels, Calvert focused on the adhesive luggage labels; it was her first official solo project and her first project involving hand lettering. Because the company's staff spoke so many languages, Margaret's system used colours, letters, and numbers to make the labels easy to decipher.

Next, the Anderson committee, which was masterminding the creation of Britain's first motorways, commissioned the firm to design a new road-sign system. Because drivers would now be able to drive faster than ever, the signs would need to be read and understood in an instant.

Above and below: Calvert's signage on the M6 in Lancashire, UK and, below, her iconic road sign for a nearby school

Calvert and Kinneir developed a new typeface, Transport, influenced by the sans-serif typeface Akzidenz-Grotesk. This was controversial because it used both upper- and lower-case letters in the designs, rather than the block text that was standard at the time. The reasoning was that a mixture of upper-case and lower-case letters forms a recognizable shape, while text based on capitals simply forms a rectangle, making words more difficult to discern from a distance.

The letters were set out in a tile system to make sure the spacing was consistent. The signs themselves were often three times larger than previous versions, leading to complaints that they were too big. But Calvert and Kinneir held their ground, and once put into production, their road signs proved hugely effective. While they have been modified slightly over the years, their design system remains largely unchanged.

The rest of the road system, however, remained untouched. In 1961, typographer Herbert Spencer published a photographic article about the unholy mess of signage he saw while driving from Marble Arch to Heathrow, some 15 miles away—a confused jumble of shapes, colours, and fonts. He was not alone in his disquiet. The Worboys Committee was formed by the British government in July 1963 to review signage on all British roads, and it commissioned Calvert and Kinneir to develop a new standardized system.

Calvert came up with simple, easy-to-understand pictograms, including the signs for "men at work" (showing a man digging), "farm animals" (showing a cow), and "schoolchildren nearby" (a girl, whom she modelled after herself, leading a boy by the hand). Shape and colour were also important. For instance, rectangular signs relayed general information, such as street names. Primary roads used yellow lettering for road numbers on a green background, while secondary routes used black lettering against a white background.

MARGARET CALVERT

In 1964 Calvert was promoted to partner at the firm, which was renamed Kinneir Calvert Associates. The new road-network signs were officially launched in 1965 and had a huge impact on highway signage worldwide.

Over the next 20 years, Calvert and Kinneir continued to shape the look of Britain's transport signage. Their designs for the rail system feature the neo-Grotesque sans-serif typeface Rail Alphabet, which was implemented in design guidelines across 2,000 stations, 45 ships, 4,000 locomotives, and 230,000 passenger carriages before privatization in 1994 led to a diversity of new corporate identities. In 2020, Calvert partnered with typographer Henrik Kubel to adapt this system as Rail Alphabet 2, a graphic identity for Network Rail stations and digital text.

In the 1980s Calvert's eponymous slab-serif font, designed for the Tyne and Wear Metro system, represented a shift from the sans-serif typeface used in transport signage. She felt it reflected Newcastle's distinctive architecture, and today it remains in use on the Metro as well as on buses and ferries in the northeast. It originated in a rejected 1970s proposal as a visual identity for the French new town of Saint Quentin-en-Yvelines.

In 1987 Calvert was appointed head of graphic design at the Royal College of Art, where she taught until 1991. In 2011 she was made a Royal Designer for Industry, and in 2015 she was presented with the D&AD President's Award, its highest honour. A retrospective exhibition of her work, *Margaret Calvert: Woman at Work*, was held from October 2020 until January 2021 at the Design Museum in London.

Her lasting legacy will be her work on road signage, which remains as eminently functional and legible as when it was introduced. "I liked the importance of it," she told the design blog It's Nice That in 2019. "This was England rebuilding after the war, with the motorways. And to be working on such an important job and meeting with architects and all these designers who were making it all happen—that was the late '50s and '60s for me. And yes, absolutely, I thought this is something worthwhile."

"...I THOUGHT THIS IS SOMETHING WORTHWHILE"

Margaret Calvert

Left: The Calvert slab-serif font, designed for the Tyne and Wear Metro system in the UK

Above: Weltformat poster for the Graphic Design Festival in Lucerne, Switzerland

ROSMARIE TISSI

"HER WORK WAS, AND STILL IS, ELEGANT AND POWERFUL, ANALYTICAL AND INTUITIVE, MODERN AND POST-MODERN, ALL AT ONCE."

Paula Scher

SWISS
B. 1937

HIGHLIGHTS
Posters, typefaces

CHARACTERISTICS
Combining Swiss formalism with playful experimentation

A number of great designers in the second half of the 20th century were influenced by the Swiss Style: a systemic approach to graphic design that emerged in Switzerland during the 1950s. But few of them have evolved that style in such new, interesting, and experimental directions as Rosmarie Tissi, who is best known for her bright and colourful poster designs.

As the website Designing Women put it: "[Her] style has been evolving throughout her career, from the pure functionality of grid-based Modernist design to a very individualistic aesthetic with vivid colours, peculiar proportions and experimental layouts."

Tissi was born in 1937 in Thayngen, Switzerland. In 1953 she spent a year studying at the Kunstgewerbeschule (School of Arts and Crafts) in Zurich. As well as learning about Swiss Style, she discovered American designers including Saul Bass (page 72), Gene Federico, and George Tscherny through magazines such as *Graphis*.

After that she landed a four-year apprenticeship with designer Siegfried Odermatt, who was known for his bold style and rebellious attitude toward industry rules. The pair worked on print and type projects, mostly for cultural institutes and publishing houses.

Above: Two poster designs for the 31st Jazz Festival, Schaffhausen

In 1957 Tissi's work was published for the first time, in *Neue Grafik*, a quarterly graphic-design journal; it was a poster she'd made for the autumn fair in her home village. She completed her apprenticeship the following year. In 1968 she became Odermatt's business partner, and the company was renamed O&T. Over time they also became a couple.

However, their collaboration was based on mutual criticism rather than a shared mindset. They each had their own individual style and approach, so they worked separately and exchanged feedback along the way.

In an interview for the TM RSI SGM 1960–90 Research Archive, Tissi recalled these years as a dream era for designers, who had wide creative freedom in interpreting commercial briefs. "Those years, the 1960s and '70s, until the '80s, were wonderful because clients wanted to have good design and they had money," she said. "Then suddenly clients wanted to save money and started to ask, 'Why is this not red?' and things like that. Before that, you could just do good work and clients didn't try to change it."

Tissi took this creative freedom and ran with it, working mostly for Swiss clients and breathing new life into constructive graphics through playful interactions among composition, colour, and typography.

Of all her posters, Tissi's personal favourite is her Zurich concert series, Serenades. The designs bring the bright and cheerful sound that characterizes a serenade to visual life through simple geometric shapes that provide both tension and balance.

She is also known for making inventive use of lettering. This was exemplified in her 1986 ad for Belgian journal Tips, which features an eye-catching letter montage; and in her letterhead for Art Garage gallery, which transformed the letter G so much that it became four circles symbolizing the wheels of a car.

Tissi's work also includes logos, textbooks, banknotes, and typefaces. One of her most famous typefaces was Sinaloa, created in 1972. A logotype-style typeface with strong geometric forms, each character has a striped stroke that helps keep the letters legible while giving them an eye-catching appearance. Another notable typeface was Mindanao (1975), which was revived in digital form in 2019 as HFF Warped Zone.

With a curious spirit and relentless work ethic, Tissi has continued to evolve her style. While her early work is characterized by the pure functionality of grid-based Modernist design, she gradually developed an individualistic aesthetic known for its vivid colours, geometric shapes, offbeat proportions, experimental layouts, and a sense of playfulness.

Above: Poster design for the International Music Festival in Lucerne

"I HAVE ALWAYS REDUCED MY DESIGN TO THE ESSENTIAL..."

Rosmarie Tissi

ROSMARIE TISSI

Right: Poster for a concert in Zurich's Park der Villa Schönberg

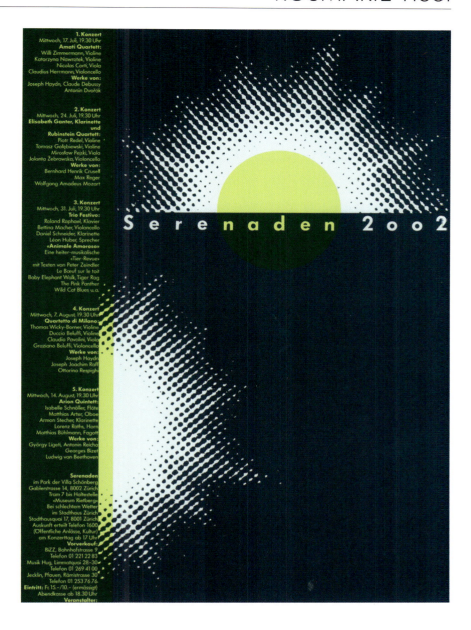

At the same time she remains wedded to most of the principles of minimalism and functionality that form the core of the Swiss Style philosophy. She said, "I have always reduced my design to the essential, employed only a few elements and played with the proportions and the empty spaces." Her work was, in other words, too abstract to be strictly Swiss, while being too Swiss to be mistaken for something else.

Tissi has been awarded numerous prizes, including three Swiss Federal Scholarships for Applied Arts; first prize and a gold medal at the 11th International Poster Biennial in Warsaw in 1986; and second prize at the competition for a new Swiss bank-note design in 1989. Alongside her professional practice she has taught and lectured at the Rhode Island School of Design and Yale University, and been a member of several juries for design competitions in Germany, Japan, Switzerland, and the US. Her work is included in the permanent collections of the Museum of Modern Art, Die Neue Sammlung in Munich, the German Poster Museum in Essen, and the Ginza Graphic Gallery in Tokyo.

Currently living and working in Zurich, Tissi remains a beacon for designers by demonstrating that the principles of Modernism can coexist with fun, playfulness, and creative flair. In the words of Paula Scher (see Chapter 34), "Her work was, and still is, elegant and powerful, analytical and intuitive, modern and post-modern, all at once."

GIORGETTO GIUGIARO

GIUGIARO IS, BY GENERAL CONSENT, THE MOST INFLUENTIAL CAR DESIGNER ALIVE.

He was the creative visionary behind an endless stream of iconic cars, including the Fiat Uno and the VW Golf. And even if you can't tell a Ford from a Fiat, most people will at least recognize his body design for the DeLorean, as seen in the Back to the Future movies.

Giugiaro was born in Garessio, Italy. His family was an artistic one; his father, grandfather, and great-grandfather were all painters. In 1952 his family moved to Turin, the centre of the country's car industry,

ITALIAN
B. 1938

HIGHLIGHTS
Car design, product design

CHARACTERISTICS
Artistry, attention to detail, experimentation

Opposite: The design classic, Volkswagen Golf

where he enrolled in the design school of the famous 1920s caricaturist known as Golia. At an end-of-term party, he met Golia's nephew Dante Giacosa, Fiat's chief engineer. Giacosa saw Giugiaro's car drawings and offered him an apprenticeship at Fiat.

In 1955 Giugiaro was hired at the Fiat Special Vehicles Styling Center in Turin, but over the next four years his supervisor refused to present any of his projects to the chief. Thankfully, he was headhunted by automobile designer Giuseppe "Nuccio" Bertone, who hired him as chief design consultant at his company, Carrozzeria Bertone, on almost double his previous pay. Bertone gave him a test design, which later became the Alfa Romeo 2000.

Awarded broad creative freedom in his new role, Giugiaro quickly developed a reputation for popular designs with vehicles such as the ASA 1000, Alfa Romeo 2000/2600 Sprint coupé, Giulia Sprint coupé, BMW 3200 CS coupé, Iso Rivolta, Simca 1000 Coupé, and Mazda 1500.

His reputation was further cemented by the Ferrari 250 GT, a one-off two-seater coupé that is distinctively different from most other Ferraris; the Chevrolet Corvair Testudo, which set the template for several cars that followed; and the Alfa Romeo Canguro, a concept car with a body made of fibreglass rather than aluminium. While no two designs were the same, each one was characterized by meticulous attention to detail and an innate artistry. They often also demonstrated Giugiaro's willingness to innovate and experiment with style and materials.

In 1965 Giugiaro left Bertone and joined Ghia, where he developed the Maserati Ghibli and the De Tomaso Mangusta. Three years later he opened his own studio with engineer Aldo Mantovani. He called it Ital Styling, and later Italdesign.

Other classic designs followed, including the Bizzarrini Manta, Alfa Romeo Iguana, Alfa Romeo Caimano, and Maserati Boomerang. The company's reputation was further enhanced by projects such as the Alfasud, Alfasud Sprint, and Alfetta GTV coupé for Alfa Romeo as well as the Golf, Scirocco, and Passat for Volkswagen.

In 1972 the Boomerang, a concept car for Maserati, launched a whole new look for cars based on wedges and sharp, straight lines inspired by Japanese origami. The most famous commercial application of this "folded paper" style, though, was his own Volkswagen Golf Mk1, his most commercially successful design.

Although a commercial failure, 1981's DMC DeLorean has an iconic status among movie fans due to its central role in *Back to the Future*. Its design featured a number of unusual construction details, including gull-wing doors, unpainted stainless-steel body panels, and a rear-mounted engine. It was based on one of Giugiaro's previous creations, the Volkswagen/Porsche Tapiro, a concept car from 1970.

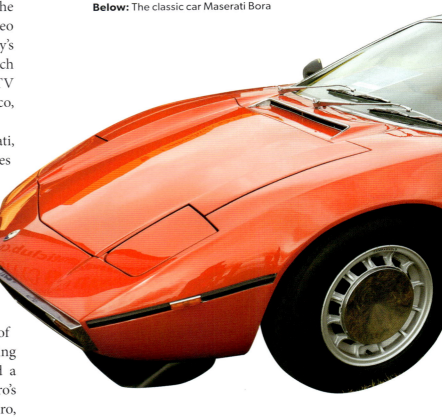

Below: The classic car Maserati Bora

Right: The DMC DeLorean, made famous by the film franchise *Back to the Future*

GIORGETTO GIUGIARO

After Italdesign was taken over by Volkswagen in 2015, Giugiaro launched a new design studio, GFG Style (for Giorgetto Fabrizio Giugiaro) with his son, Fabrizio. Their design methodology puts the emphasis on functional factors combined with comfort, reduced weight, and lower production costs by making use of the most advanced technologies and efficient energy use.

Giugiaro was named Car Designer of the Century in 1999, and was inducted into the Automotive Hall of Fame in Detroit in 2002.

"IT WASN'T AN ARCHITECT OR DESIGNER WHO INVENTED OBJECTS, BUT AN ARTISAN."
Giorgetto Giugiaro

All in all, over four decades, Giugiaro and his team at Italdesign designed over 200 products, including the Lotus Esprit and the BMW M1. Perhaps the most outlandish was the Lancia Megagamma in 1978, a high-riding proto-minivan that evolved from his 1976 Alfa design for the New York "taxi of tomorrow." It wasn't a success, but arguably acted as a precursor to the MPV/minivan.

Giugiaro didn't just design cars. Over the years, he also designed camera bodies for Nikon; the Seiko Speedmaster wristwatch; a high-speed tilting train; a 17-metre yacht; the navigation promenade of Porto Santo Stefano, on the west coast of Italy; Lausanne Cathedral's organ; a new pasta shape called Marille; office furniture for Okamura; and the official basketball of the International Basketball Federation.

He is also considered a thought leader. He has given well-received speeches at the International Design Conference in Aspen, Colorado, and the world congresses of the International Council of Societies of Industrial Design in Milan and Nagoya, as well as a report on the future of cars to the Assises Mondiales de l'Automobile in Paris. In 1985 he was elected to the Management Committee of the Italian Industrial Design Association and held a course on design at the Faculty of Architecture in Turin.

Right: Seiko x Giugiaro wristwatch, one of many successful luxury collaborations

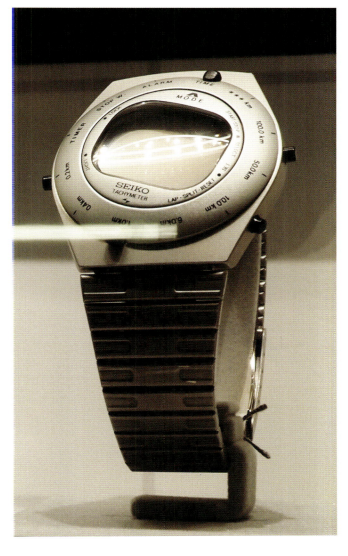

JAMES DYSON

"AN EXPERT THINKS HE KNOWS IT ALL."

James Dyson

BRITISH
B. 1947

HIGHLIGHTS
Ballbarrow, Dual Cyclone vacuum cleaner, Airblade

CHARACTERISTICS
Innovative product design that solves everyday problems

Opposite: James Dyson with a Dyson Pure Cool Smart Air Purifier in the foreground

If you ask a designer to explain the difference between art and design, they'll usually respond with something along these lines: art aims to inspire; design aims to solve problems. And if you're looking for an example of a problem solver, you can't go wrong with James Dyson. He's spent more than 50 years seeing problems, identifying solutions and then putting them into practice.

Dyson was born in 1947 in Cromer, Norfolk, one of three children. He went to the independent boarding school Gresham's from 1956 to 1965, the year his father, a headmaster, died of prostate cancer. He spent one year (1965–1966) at the Byam Shaw School of Art in London, now part of Central Saint Martins. He then studied furniture and interior design at the Royal College of Art (1966–1970) before moving into engineering, due in part to the tutelage of structural engineer Anthony Hunt.

In his final year, Dyson worked at Rotork Controls in Bath, where he worked for Jeremy Fry, an unconventional boss who encouraged young people to be innovative. Despite having no product-design experience, Dyson worked with Fry to design the Sea Truck, a flat-hulled, high-speed watercraft.

His first original creation was inspired by a wheelbarrow he saw getting stuck in the mud. Ballbarrow was a modified version of a wheelbarrow with a spherical plastic ball instead of a wheel. This made it more stable, lighter and easier to manoeuvre than a traditional wheelbarrow.

This was followed by the Trolleyball, a trolley that launched boats; and the Wheelboat, which could travel across land and water. When he filed the patent for the Wheelboat, though, he was not granted permission to commercialize the technology as it was deemed to be of military significance. A version of his design was later used by Egyptian troops to get across the Suez Canal during the 1973 Yom Kippur War.

Left: An advertisement for Dyson's first ever creation, the Ballbarrow

121

Above: A Dyson vaccum cleaner which depensed with bags

In 1978 Dyson became frustrated with the poor performance of his domestic vacuum cleaner, a Hoover Junior, as it kept getting clogged with dirt, reducing its suction. He had the idea of using cyclonic separation to create a vacuum cleaner that would not lose suction as it picked up dirt.

His inspiration came from an industrial cyclone tower that separates paint particles from the air using centrifugal force. He put his theory into practice by ripping off his Hoover's bag and replacing it with a crude cardboard prototype of his cyclone design—and it worked.

However, the directors of his Ballbarrow company—which he had founded but no longer owned—retorted that if it were possible to make a better vacuum cleaner, Hoover or Electrolux would have done so. Dyson was ultimately removed from the company. He proceeded to launch a new firm, Dyson Research Limited, which he funded with the help of one backer, his buyout funds from Ballbarrow, a second mortgage and his wife's wages as an art teacher.

The idea took five years to develop, but finally Dyson launched the G-Force in 1983. However, no manufacturer or distributor would handle his product in the UK; they made too much money from selling bags. Some also found it difficult to believe that people would want to see the dirt a vacuum cleaner had sucked up from their carpet.

Instead, Dyson launched the G-Force through catalogue sales in Japan. Its high-tech form, eye-catching colours and ability to provide continuous suction made it a success, despite it being expensive, and it won Japan's 1991 International Design Fair prize.

Based on this achievement, Dyson secured a bank loan to build his own factory in Wiltshire, in the west of England. The (possibly apocryphal) story goes that the bank manager's wife had tried out the vacuum cleaner at home and loved it. The DA001, later renamed the DC01, launched in Britain in 1993; the letters stood for Dual Cyclone. Its slogan—"Say goodbye to the bag"—grabbed attention, and it became the top-selling vacuum cleaner in Britain despite a retail price considerably higher than that of competing brands.

He licensed the technology in North America from 1986 to 2001, after which he entered the market directly. By 2005 his vacuum cleaners had reportedly become the market leaders in the United States by value.

"SAY GOODBYE TO THE BAG."

James Dyson

JAMES DYSON

Another landmark design, the Dyson Airblade, came in 2006. It was a fast hand dryer that used a thin sheet of moving air as a squeegee to remove water, rather than attempting to evaporate it with heat. This meant it dried faster and used less energy than traditional hand dryers. The Airblade was followed in 2009 by the Air Multiplier, a bladeless fan that draws air through its base unit and blows it over the inner surface of an airfoil-shaped ring.

All these creations and more changed people's everyday lives in small but important ways. But more significantly, he has encouraged generations of product designers to think beyond iterating what already exists and consider building something new and revolutionary.

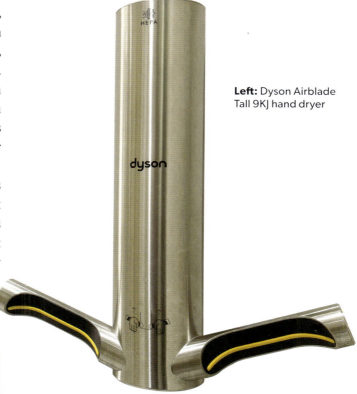

Left: Dyson Airblade Tall 9KJ hand dryer

Below: Dyson AirWrap Complete Long Volumise Hair Styler

With this in mind, in 1997 he published his autobiography, *Against the Odds*; co-written with Giles Coren, the book was an account of his persistence in the face of discouragement. It was followed by a second autobiography, *Invention: A Life*, in 2021.

More directly, Dyson tends to hire graduates without experience as a point of principle. "I think a lack of experience is a great help," he explained in a 2022 Q&A for designers hosted by *Wired*. "An expert thinks he knows it all. But he's also rather inhibited by his experience and knowledge, and he finds it difficult to steer off the well-trodden path."

Dyson also gets hands-on with inspiring and helping young people across the world realize their design ideas. In 2002 he established the James Dyson Foundation, which encourages young designers and engineers by awarding prizes and grants. In 2007 he launched the James Dyson Award, an international award scheme that challenges students to "design something that solves a problem."

One further quote from Dyson, in a video to promote *Invention: A Life*, probably sums up his design philosophy better than any other. "If you have a better idea and engineer it well," he said, "people will want it—even if it's three times the price."

ERIK SPIEKERMANN

SPIEKERMANN IS ONE OF THE MOST IMPORTANT TYPOGRAPHERS AND GRAPHIC DESIGNERS OF THE 20TH AND 21ST CENTURIES.

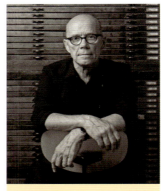

GERMAN
B. 1947

HIGHLIGHTS
Typography, visual identities, wayfinding

CHARACTERISTICS
Attention to detail, knowledge of production methods

Erik Spiekermann has had a profound impact on the way we see and use typography, and his work has helped shape the visual identity of some of the world's most recognizable brands. He's perhaps best known for the signage Germans see every day in the country's rail and air networks.

He was born in Stadthagen, Germany in 1947. He studied art history at Berlin's Freie Universität (Free University), one of the country's most prestigious educational institutions, and funded his tuition fees by running a letterpress printing press in his basement. During the 1970s he spent a decade in London, freelancing as a graphic designer for several consultancies including Filmcomposition and Wolff Olins as well as teaching at the London College of Printing. In 1976 he started designing typefaces for the Berlin foundry Berthold: LoType and Berliner Grotesk.

In 1979 he returned to Berlin and founded MetaDesign. The studio quickly established a reputation for corporate design, working for clients including Berthold, Bosch, Springer Publishing, Audi, Volkswagen, and Heidelberg Printing among others. Spiekermann's obsessive attention to detail and healthy knowledge of analogue and digital production methods earned him international respect.

Above: Spiekermann's printing studio

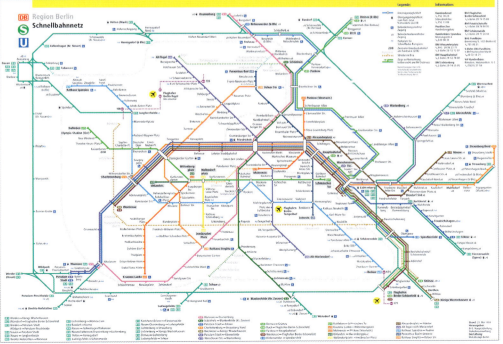

Left: The Berlin Underground map

Above: Designs for house numbers

Below: A poster showcasing typefaces

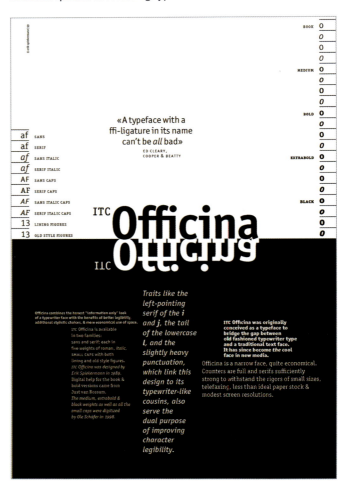

Perhaps his most lasting influence and legacy may be in his wayfinding work, notably for Berlin public transport company BVG. This was a big challenge; after the fall of the Berlin Wall and the reunification of Berlin in 1990, there was no unified information system for public transport. That year Spiekermann was commissioned to develop a new passenger information system for BVG from scratch, including fonts, symbols, layouts and colours.

Key to this effort was consistency. For example, Spiekermann introduced yellow as the sole colour for vehicles, whereas previously they had been white, grey, beige, yellow, orange or red. The studio also designed Transit, a custom typeface for signage based on Frutiger Condensed (it was published commercially in 1997 as FF Transit).

In 1989 he and his then-wife, Joan, launched FontShop, the first mail order retailer for electronic fonts. Then in 1991 the couple partnered with English graphic designer Neville Brody to start an independent type foundry, FontShop International (FSI).

FSI's main focus was the extension and maintenance of its typeface library, which was called FontFont. Notable typefaces include Spiekermann's FF Meta, FF Unit, FF Info, FF Real, as well as many faces by well-known designers like Martin Majoor, Mike Abbink, Christian Schwartz, Erik van Blokland, Just van Rossum, Albert Jan Pool, and many young designers who published their first typefaces with

ERIK SPIEKERMANN

the FF label. FSI also published FontBook, an independent compendium of digital typefaces, and 18 issues of the experimental typographical magazine FUSE. It first organized the FUSE conferences in 1995— forerunners of the annual European design conference TYPO Berlin.

"I'm obviously a typomaniac, which is an incurable if not mortal disease," Spiekermann said in the 2007 documentary *Helvetica*. "I can't explain it… I just like looking at type. I just get a total kick out of it. They are my friends."

Meanwhile, MetaDesign went from strength to strength, opening offices in San Francisco (1992), London (1995) and Zurich (2000). However, Spiekermann left MetaDesign over policy disagreements and in 2002 started United Designers Network, later Edenspiekermann, which opened offices in Berlin, Los Angeles and San Francisco.

In 1993 he published a book on typography, *Stop Stealing Sheep & Find Out How Type Works*, which has been published in four editions since then. In 2001 he redesigned British magazine *The Economist*; its circulation went from 500,000 to almost 1 million by the end of the following year. In 2001–2002 he designed a corporate font family for Nokia.

His family of typefaces for Deutsche Bahn (German Railways), designed with Christian Schwartz, received a gold medal in 2006 at the German Federal Design Prize, the highest such award in Germany. In 2007 he was the first designer to be elected to the European Design Awards Hall of Fame, and in 2009 he was named European Ambassador for Innovation and Creativity by the European Union. He was declared Royal Designer for Industry title from the British Royal Society of Arts in 2007.

Spiekermann received the German National Design award for a Personality in 2011. In 2013 he designed Fira Sans for Firefox OS in collaboration with Carrois Type Design. A book about him by Johannes Erler in a German (Hallo ich bin Erik) and an English edition (Hello I am Erik) was published in 2014.

In 2014 he set up Hacking Gutenberg, an experimental letterpress workshop in Berlin which explores how letterpress can be redefined in the 21st century through research, printing, collecting, publishing and making things. The workshop has several proof- and platen presses as well as other traditional analogue equipment, lots of wood and metal type, a Ludlow caster, a Risograph, a Glowforge laser. They built their own laser to make polymer metal-backed 50×70cm (20×28") plates direct from digital data and print those plates on a 1954 Heidelberg Cylinder letterpress.

In 2023, he partnered with Alexander Roth to revive Berthold's Akzidenz Grotesk Serie 57, a metal typeface he found in a case in his workshop which had never been digitized. Their version was published as neue Serie57. It was awarded a gold medal at the German Federal Design Prize that year.

Spiekermann continues to be involved with both analogue and digital projects, including consulting with his former studio, Edenspiekermann, and with Applied Wayfinding in London on large and complex wayfinding systems around the world.

PAULA SCHER

HER STORY IS AN INSPIRATION FOR ANYONE ARTISTIC WHO EVER DOUBTED THEMSELVES.

AMERICAN
B. 1948

HIGHLIGHTS
Logo design, visual identity, typography, album covers

CHARACTERISTICS
Simple visual solutions to complex problems

Opposite: Philadelphia Explained, Tyler School of Art, Temple University, Philadephia, USA

"I was pretty terrible at almost everything I did in art school," Paula Scher told *Madame Architect* magazine in 2017. "There were people who drew better than me, painted better than me, sculpted better than me, everything." Yet she went on to become the first female partner at Pentagram, and to create some of the most influential logos and visual identities in modern graphic-design history.

She was born in 1948, in Washington, D.C. Her father, who worked for the US Geological Survey as a photogrammetric engineer, invented a device that corrects the distortion caused by aerial photography. At school she made paper dolls and comic strips for fun. As a teenager she took art classes at Corcoran College of Art and Design, and as publicity chairman of her high school she designed posters for proms and other events.

Despite her father's opposition, Scher went to study at the Tyler School of Art in Pennsylvania, where she fell in love with typography. She received a Bachelor of Fine Arts degree in 1970. She also got a teaching certificate, in case she didn't make it as an artist.

Scher moved to New York City and took her first job as a layout artist for Random House's children's book division. However, in 1972 she heard her boss was leaving, and feared she'd lose her job. So she called up a friend working in the promotions department at CBS Records and ended up working there for two years.

Below: Poster design for jazz musicians Bob James and Earl Klugh

Her next job was as art director for Atlantic Records, where she designed her first album covers. A year later, she returned to CBS as art director for its cover department. Over the next eight years, Scher designed up to 150 album covers a year.

She became known for reviving historical typefaces and design styles, and was particularly influenced by Art Nouveau and Constructivism. She began to develop a style of decorative typography integrated with imagery, which she normally commissioned because she didn't think her illustration was good enough. Four of her covers were nominated for Grammys: *One on One* by Bob James and Earl Klugh; *Heads* by Bob James, *Favorites* by the Yardbirds; and *Ginseng Woman* by Eric Gale.

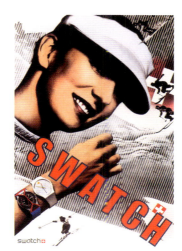

Above: An advertisement for Swatch watches

In 1984 she co-founded Koppel & Scher, a design partnership with editorial designer Terry Koppel, whom she knew from the Tyler School of Art. Over the next seven years, she designed corporate identities, packaging, book jackets, and ads, including a famous Swatch poster. It featured a smiling visor-clad woman brandishing a disembodied arm that bears two Swatch watches against a background of skiers; it was a parody of a famous 1930s poster designed by Herbert Matter for the Swiss National Tourist Office.

In 1991 the studio was affected by the economic downturn, and Koppel went to work for *Esquire* magazine. Scher began consulting, then joined design consultancy Pentagram as a partner. She has been a principal at the New York office ever since.

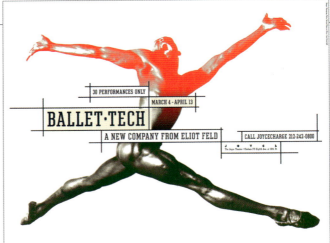

Left: A poster advertising Public Theater's 95/96 season

Above: An advertising poster for a new ballet company

Pentagram has a unique place in the annals of graphic design. Founded in London in 1972, it has evolved over the years with offices across the UK, Europe, and the US. It's revered in the profession for two main reasons: its critically acclaimed work and its unusual structure, in which a hierarchically flat group of partners own and manage the firm, often working collaboratively, and share in profits and decision-making.

During her time at Pentagram, Scher has developed a dizzying array of identity and branding systems, promotional materials, environmental graphics, packaging, and publication designs for a broad range of clients including Bloomberg, Microsoft, Coca-Cola, MoMA, the Sundance Institute, the Metropolitan Opera, the New York City Ballet, the New York Philharmonic, the New Jersey Performing Arts Center, the United States Holocaust Memorial Museum, the Philadelphia Museum of Art, and the New York City Department of Parks and Recreation.

Above: The logo for Citi Bank, reimagined by Scher

To do her achievements at Pentagram justice would require a book (which does, in fact, exist: *Paula Scher: Works*). But a few highlights will offer some insight into why she is so respected.

In 1994 she created a new, unified visual identity for the Public Theater in New York. To attract a more diverse demographic, she created a graphic language that incorporated street typography and graffiti-like juxtapositions. She was also inspired by Rob Roy Kelly's American Wood Type and posters from theatre in Victorian London. This fusion of high and low became a huge influence on theatrical promotion, and on cultural institutions in general.

In 1998 financial giants Citicorp and Travelers Group merged to create Citigroup, the largest financial company in the world. According to a widely reported story, Pentagram was paid $1.5m to develop its visual identity, and during their first meeting, Scher sketched what was to become their ubiquitous logo on the back of a napkin in five minutes.

This is not to say (as many articles have implied) that she earned $1.5m for five minutes' work. There is always more to developing a corporate identity than just a sketch—and in this case there were two more years of development. But it does highlight Scher's genius in distilling complex design challenges into simple, effective solutions.

PAULA SCHER

"I LOVE THE BIG SCALE AND IMMEDIATE IMPACT OF POSTERS. THEY'RE MY FAVOURITE THINGS TO DESIGN."

Here's another example: In 2012 Scher created a new logo for Windows 8 that took it back to its roots as a window. Early in the development process, Scher asked, "Your name is Windows. Why are you a flag?" Her new design reimagined the company's old four-colour symbol as a more modern geometric shape.

Not only has Scher inspired generations of designers with her work, she has also been keen to share her process and ideas through teaching, conferences, and interviews. She has taught at the School of Visual Arts in New York for over two decades, and has also held positions at Cooper Union, Yale University, and the Tyler School of Art. A select member of Alliance Graphique Internationale, Scher has had her work included in the collections of MoMA, the Library of Congress in Washington, D.C., the Museum für Gestaltung, Zurich, and the Centre Georges Pompidou. She has also received more than 300 awards from international design associations as well as prizes from the American Institute of Graphic Design, The Type Directors Club, the Art Directors Club of New York, and the Package Design Council.

She lives and works in New York, and was profiled in the first season of the Netflix documentary series *Abstract: The Art of Design*.

Below: Scher's design for Achievement First Endeavor Middle School in Brooklyn, 2010

LONNIE JOHNSON

"WHEN I WAS A KID, I ALWAYS WANTED TO MAKE A BETTER TOY."

The word "designer" isn't the first most people use to describe Lonnie Johnson. He's usually referred to as an inventor, aerospace engineer, or entrepreneur.

Yet a designer he clearly is. And despite the importance of his science and engineering contributions, he's probably best known for designing one of the world's best-selling toys: the Super Soaker water gun.

He was born Lonnie George Johnson in Mobile, Alabama, in 1949. His mother was a nurse's aide and his father was a World War II veteran who worked as a civilian driver on local air bases. He taught his son how electricity worked and how to fix household appliances such as steam irons.

As a child Johnson was an inveterate tinkerer, and once pulled apart his sister's baby doll to see what made its eyes close. He also tried to create rocket fuel in a saucepan and almost burned down the family home. The neighbourhood kids nicknamed him "The Professor," and he once built a working engine out of parts from a scrapyard and used it to power a go-kart.

As a black child growing up during segregation, Johnson was warned by his teachers not to aspire to a career in science. However, inspired by the example of George Washington Carver, one of the most prominent black scientists of the early 20th century, he ignored them.

AMERICAN
B. 1949

HIGHLIGHTS
Super Soaker water gun

CHARACTERISTICS
Applied science and engineering to design one of the world's most popular toys

Left: Lonnie Johnson with the patent for his Super Soaker water gun

> "THE ONLY THING ANYBODY FROM THE UNIVERSITY SAID TO US WAS, 'GOODBYE' AND 'Y'ALL DRIVE SAFE, NOW'."

In 1968 Johnson represented his high school at a science fair. It was held at the University of Alabama at Tuscaloosa, where, five years earlier, Governor George Wallace had tried to prevent two black students from enrolling. Johnson won a prize for presenting a robot built from junkyard scraps and powered by compressed air. He was, however, the only black student in attendance. He later recalled, "The only thing anybody from the university said to us during the entire competition was, 'Goodbye' and 'Y'all drive safe, now.'"

The following year, Johnson attended Tuskegee University, a private, historically black land-grant university in Alabama. He completed a B.S. in mechanical engineering in 1973 and a master's degree in nuclear engineering in 1975. After graduating, he worked for the US Air Force on the stealth bomber program before joining NASA's Jet Propulsion Laboratory in 1979. Over the next 12 years, he contributed to a variety of projects, including the Galileo mission to Jupiter, and the *Mariner Mark II* Spacecraft series.

In 1991 he left NASA and founded his own company, Johnson Research and Development Co. He currently has three technology-development companies: Excellatron Solid State, Johnson Energy Storage, and Johnson Electro-Mechanical Systems. He has also been working on the Johnson Thermoelectric Energy Converter, or JTEC, an engine that converts heat directly into electricity, which could eventually provide a low-cost way to create solar power.

In short, Johnson has both helped humanity explore the universe and worked to solve environmental problems. But ultimately he'll be remembered for something quite different: redesigning the water gun.

The water gun, aka squirt gun, had been around a long time. The first known reference is from General William T. Sherman during the Civil War in 1861. Johnson, however, raised it to a whole new level with his groundbreaking design for the Super Soaker, originally called the Power Drencher.

Before then, the standard approach to water guns was piston-based; these guns don't have triggers, but are fired simply by pumping, giving them limited range and power. Johnson's design, in contrast, is pressurized by air being pumped and compressed into a large reservoir. When the trigger is pulled, a valve is opened and the compressed air pushes the water out of the nozzle.

Left: Lonnie Johnson at one of his technology-development facilities

Opposite: The Super Soaker water gun, which is the most well-known of all of Lonnie Johnson's inventions

LONNIE JOHNSON

"I KNEW IT WOULD BE SUCCESSFUL. I DID NOT REALISE HOW SUCCESSFUL IT WOULD BE."

He originally got the idea in 1982 while experimenting with a new type of refrigeration system that would use water rather than CFCs. One day he machined a nozzle and hooked it up to the bathroom sink, and it shot out a powerful stream of water, giving Johnson an instant burst of childish glee. Several months later he built a prototype of a pressurized water gun in his basement using Plexiglas, PVC pipe, O-ring seals and a two-litre soda bottle for the reservoir.

Johnson then spent seven years trying to arrange partnerships with toy companies to bring the product to market. Finally, in 1989, he successfully pitched to Larami after demonstrating his prototype at its headquarters in Philadelphia. He worked with Larami design director William Raucci and engineering consultant Bruce D'Andrade to make a version of the gun that could be mass-produced.

The first commercial version was released in 1990 and was a huge success. It generated $200m in sales in 1991, helping him fund Johnson R&D. That year he also launched the Super Soaker 100, a version that incorporated a separate air chamber.

Since then Johnson has continued to produce newer and better designs under the Super Soaker brand. For example, the Quick Blast, his first spring-loaded water gun, was launched in 2008. In 2011 he released the Thunderstorm, which used an electric pump to push water directly out of the nozzle. Then in 2013 came the Flash Blast, which has a trigger mechanism similar to a Nerf gun.

In total, more than 170 models of Super Soaker have been launched. In 2015 it was inducted into the National Toy Hall of Fame and, according to Hasbro, it's currently approaching sales of $1 billion.

Johnson lives and works in Atlanta, Georgia. He has been given numerous honours and awards, and in 2022 was inducted into the National Inventors Hall of Fame.

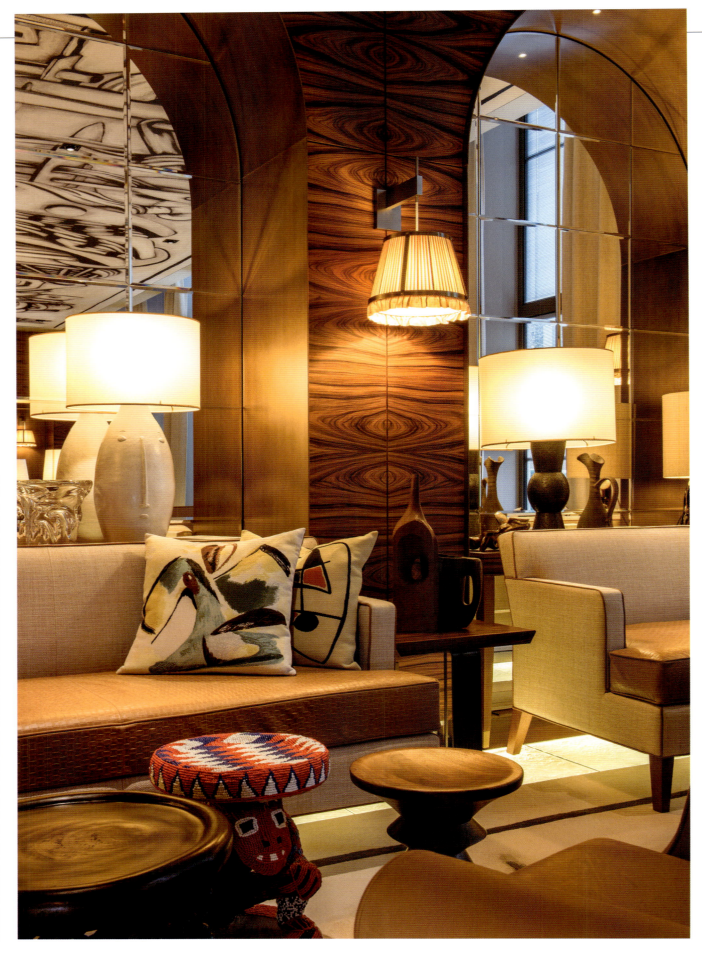

PHILIPPE STARCK

STARCK IS CELEBRATED AS ONE OF THE WORLD'S GREATEST LIVING CREATORS.

FRENCH
B. 1949

HIGHLIGHTS
Industrial design, furniture design, interior design

CHARACTERISTICS
Precision, luxurious, timeless

Left: A.I, chair, Autodesk and Kartell, 2017

Opposite: The Brach hotel, Paris, France, 2018

Philippe Starck is one of the most prolific designers alive today, with more than 10,000 individual designs to his name. He is also one of the most eclectic, working across industrial design, architecture, interior design, street furniture, household appliances, office automation, lighting, clothing, transport, naval and spatial engineering. What unites this diverse work is his passionate belief that creation, whatever form it takes, must improve the lives of as many people as possible.

Starck was born in Paris in 1949. His father was an aeronautical engineer and inventor who told him that invention was a duty. "[He] left me with the idea that one of the most beautiful jobs you can do is a creative job," Starck recalled. "And by creating airplanes, he taught me some precious things: to make a plane fly you have to create it, but to keep it from falling you have to be rigorous."

After studying at the Ecole Nissim de Camondo, he founded in 1979 his own design company, Starck Product, which he later renamed Ubik after the novel by Philip K. Dick. This led to collaborations with the biggest design manufacturers in Italy including Driade, Alessi, and Kartell as well as international clients such as Drimmer in Austria, Vitra in Switzerland, and Disform in Spain.

In the 1980s, he went on to design many restaurant interiors worldwide including Café Costes in Paris, Manin in Tokyo, Peninsula Felix in Hong Kong. He refurbished the private apartments in the Elysée Palace in Paris for President Mitterrand in 1983 and built a reputation for designing hotel interiors, beginning with the Royalton and Paramount hotels in New York City. A pioneer and visionary, he was the driving force behind the first Boutique Hotels, defining the concept without ever really grasping the term. Over the years, Starck's name has become synonymous with elegant and stimulating hospitality design, with many celebrated projects including Le

Left: Rabo di Galo bar, Rosewood, São Paulo

Opposite: Adela Rex, Andreu World, 2021

Below: Louis Ghost, chair, Kartell, 2000

Royal Monceau (2010), Le Meurice (2008 and 2016), Brach Paris (2018), La Reserve Eden au Lac in Zurich (2020), La Co(o)rniche in Pyla (2021), TOO hotel in Paris (2022), Rosewood Cidade Matarazzo in Sao Paulo (2022), Mondrian Bordeaux Les Carmes (2023).

Philippe Starck is also highly respected as an architect. After his first avant-garde expressionist architecture buildings with a number of commissions coming from Japan—most famously the Nani Nani (1989) and the Asahi Beer Hall (1992), he was appointed – among others – to design the control tower at Bordeaux's airport (1997), the extension of the École Nationale Supérieure des Arts Décoratifs in Paris (1998), the Alhondiga in Bilbao (2010), Port Adriano in Majorca (2012), P.A.T.H. a concept of Prefabricated Accessible Technological Homes (2014), and numerous hospitality projects such as Faena in Buenos Aires (2002), Fasano in Rio de Janeiro (2007), Le Nuage in Montpellier (2014), the Chateau Les Carmes Haut-Brion winehouse (2018), Lily of the Valley near Saint Tropez (2019), Villa M in Paris (2021), and La Almazara (2024) in Ronda, the world's first olive oil mill and museum designed by a renowned creator.

From everyday products to individual windmill, electric vehicles to highly technological medical devices, or from perfumes to organic food and clothing, Starck has an international reputation for industrial design. As a furniture designer, he is well known for pieces such as the Louis Ghost chair and the A.I chair for Kartell, the first piece of furniture to be created with the help of artificial intelligence. The Juicy Salif for Alessi, a citrus squeezer, born from Starck's reflection on a mathematical exercise of reverse topography, turning concave into convex, is still 30 years after its creation, one of the world's most sold design item.

More broadly, Starck is known for his concept of democratic design, which has led him to focus on mass-produced consumer goods rather than one-off pieces and seek ways to reduce cost and improve quality for to make 'good design' accessible to the largest number

"IF I HADN'T BECOME A DESIGNER, I WOULD PROBABLY HAVE BEEN A WRITER OR MAYBE A POLITICIAN."

Philippe Starck

PHILIPPE STARCK

of people. In 1998 he put this principle into practice by establishing the Good Goods catalogue with La Redoute, proposing 170 sustainable and respectful everyday "non-products for non-consumers of the future moral market". In 2000 he worked with Target and proposed a collection of more than 50 products that represented his democratic design ideals.

Starck told *The Guardian* in 2013 that he was only interested in the impact he had on the world through the service he could give to his community. "If I hadn't become a designer, I would probably have been a writer or maybe a politician," he said.

Believing that solutions should be looked for everywhere, Philippe Starck is working on various extraterrestrial projects, among which the Axiom Space station's crew quarter habitation module and, with Orbite, on the first commercial space-flight training campus in North America.

Starck has long been a keen advocate of sustainability in all his creation by using as little material and energy as possible. For instance, all Kartell by Starck creations is produced in bio-plastics, his Broom chair for Emeco in 2012 was made from waste materials collected in lumber and plastic factories. Similarly, his 2021 Adela Rex armchair for the Spanish brand Andreu World used oak and walnut plywood he sourced from reforested land. All architectural projects are conceived with high durability and sustainability at heart, with constructions aiming toward zero impact on the ground.

By employing his prolific work across all domains, Philippe Starck continually pushes the boundaries and requirements of design, celebrated by more than 250 awards, becoming one of the most visionary and renowned creators of the international contemporary scene.

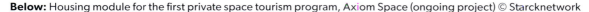

Below: Housing module for the first private space tourism program, Axiom Space (ongoing project) © Starcknetwork

PAOLA NAVONE

HER CRAFTED DESIGNS FOR EVERYDAY PRODUCTS ARE INSPIRED BY THE EAST AS MUCH AS THE WEST.

ITALIAN
B. 1950

HIGHLIGHTS
Product design, architecture, interior design, set design

CHARACTERISTICS
Mixing global influences, avant-garde approach

Left: Reichenbach Koi Koi, 2022

Opposite: Crate & Barrel Indigo Teak Console

In today's connected world, design is increasingly global. Yet most designers in the West remain primarily influenced by Western traditions. Paola Navone is one of the exceptions. Having lived and worked all over the world, she incorporates multiple global influences in her designs and, as a result of this, she produces work that is truly cosmopolitan and groundbreaking.

Navone was born in Turin, Italy, in 1950. As a student she was interested in design, but at the time there were no design schools, so she studied architecture at the Politecnico di Torino (Polytechnic University of Turin).

However, formal study wasn't enough to feed her curiosity and intellect. She travelled widely in order to collect fresh creative influences, from London to Austria to the US. Eventually she combined these discoveries into a university thesis, *Architettura Radicale* (*Radical Architecture*), which focused on avant-garde collectives.

After graduating in 1973 she moved to Milan, where she met an ethnologist in a bar. He was about to travel to Cameroon to study nomadic people, and she decided to accompany him. After two years in Africa she went back to Milan; then she got a call from Alessandro Mendini, the editor of *Casabella*, a high-end Italian architecture and product-design magazine, offering her a job.

Navone became part of an anti-academic movement that rejected the Modernist principles of the Bauhaus as too limiting and joyless. Her first design job came with Abet Laminati, a world leader in the production of decorative laminates. The company had launched a design competition, but instead of sending one entry, she sent 50. Navone was quickly offered a job, and ended up collaborating with the company for three decades.

Left: Imaginative and playful, the Ghost armchair for Gervasoni

Left: Housse armchair for Italian furniture company Baxter

What unifies her work is travel, and she's known for combining diverse cultural influences in inventive ways as well as sourcing unusual materials and incorporating a wide range of industrial and artisanal techniques.

As she told Home Journal in 2016, "The world is an endless source of inspiration. Even in the market just around the corner I can find something that attracts me and teases my creativity. In my head I collect images, things, colours, flavours and shapes from all over the world. When I start a new project, the right idea jumps out from this mix of visions."

From the early 1980s until 2000 Navone lived in Southeast Asia. This had a big influence on her work, especially in her use of bamboo in furniture design. More broadly, though, she imbued the different perspectives and approaches to design across East and West, and fused it into her own work.

She made her name in the design world, however, after joining Studio Alchimia, a post-radical avant-garde group founded in Milan in 1976. The group's activities included seminars, experimental video, clothing design, theatrical set design, product design, decorative arts, performance art, and architecture, and Navone worked with big personalities such as Ettore Sottsass, Andrea Branzi, and Alessandro Guerriero.

In 1983 Navone received the Osaka International Design Award. From 1985 to 1988 she was a consultant for international organizations such as UNIDO and the World Bank, and often travelled to East Asia, where she opened an office. In 1988 she won major international acclaim for the Mondo collection of handcrafted furniture, lighting, and accessories she designed for Italian company Cappellini. In the late 1980s and 1990s she served as art director for Gervasoni, an Italian furniture company founded in 1882, and designed the first collection for Giorgio Armani's home line, Armani/Casa.

Across her career, Navone's work has spanned product design, architecture, interior design, and set design, and she has never adhered to a single style.

Below: Chopsticks and holders in the Nomad tableware collection for Belgian designer homeware brand, Serax

"TRAVEL IS KIND OF MY WAY OF BREATHING."

Paola Navone

PAOLA NAVONE

"I learned a lot," she told *Surface* magazine in 2016. "Over there, I was working more on craft, because the factories in Southeast Asia were more about craft than industry. Then, when I was in Italy, I was doing more industry than craft. I've always liked both."

She is also influenced by the Thai philosophy of *tham ma da* (everyday), which involves finding new, extraordinary uses for seemingly cheap, standard, or utilitarian objects. More simply put, it's about presenting the ordinary in new and exciting ways. This approach has been particularly influential on her bold and inventive interior designs, from hotels in Miami and Phuket to private residences in Italy and France, and the Hong Kong boutique Joyce.

At the end of the 1990s she moved her design studio, Otto, to Milan. In 2000, German magazine *Architektur & Wohnen* named her Designer of the Year. She won a 2011 *Elle Deco* International Design Award for Big Bed (made by Poliform), an upholstered bed frame and headboard covered in removable fabric, eco-leather, and leather. In 2013 she oversaw Armani/Casa's debut collection of homeware, the Dinner with Friends series for Crate & Barrel.

She was included in *Interior Design* magazine's prestigious Hall of Fame in 2014.

Despite being embraced by the establishment, Navone has not mellowed or diluted her principles; she continues to take avant-garde approaches and challenge design norms. In 2019, for example, she gave seven McDonald's stores in France a new interior design centred around clashing prints and pops of colour purposely designed as an "imperfect, almost artisanal look."

Similarly, in 2023 she organized an exhibition for Milan Design Week titled *Take It Or Leave It*. Challenging the very nature of what design is, it featured hundreds of objects and curiosities, collected on Navone's travels, that could each be won in a lottery. She described the process as "a radical form of upcycling and reuse."

Above: Green ceramic fish dishs for Crate & Barrel
Below: Glass vases, also for international design company Crate & Barrel

AHN
SANG-SOO

"I SHARE WHAT I HAVE LEARNED AND THAT IN WHICH I AM MOST CONFIDENT."

KOREAN
B. 1952

HIGHLIGHTS
Reimagining of Hangeul typefaces

CHARACTERISTICS
Non-square, proportional

Opposite: Victor McLindon's illustration of Ahn Sang-soo

Typographers in the Western world have achieved great things over the years through iteration. But no one person can be said to have single-handedly changed the game. In Korea, though, things are different. Graphic and typographic designer Ahn Sang-soo can absolutely be said to have done this in the 1980s.

Ahn was born in 1952 in Chungju, a city in North Chungcheong province that is also the hometown of UN Secretary-General Ban Ki-moon. He obtained his BFA and MFA from Hongik University in Seoul. After graduating, he became an advertising designer for the company that later became LG Electronics. But he found the corporate world too restrictive for his artistic temperament, so he joined *Ggumim* magazine as an art editor in 1981 and then the magazines *Ma-dang* and *Meot* as art director in 1983. It was during this time that Ahn began examining the readability of the Korean typeface in newspapers. In 1985 he launched his own design firm, Ahn Graphics. And this is when he began his groundbreaking work on Hangeul typefaces.

Hangeul is a phonetic alphabet created in 1443 by King Sejong—the fourth monarch of the Joseon Dynasty—as an alternative to the Chinese characters that had been in use in Korea. It is thus the only alphabet in the world with a known team of inventors and an official proclamation date.

The king believed that the complexity of Chinese characters was the reason for widespread illiteracy among the people, and prevented them from presenting their demands and grievances in writing. His new, unifying, comprehensive, scientific alphabet was much simpler and more flexible, allowing the representation of regional dialects and foreign words. His innovation is celebrated annually across the country on 9 October, Hangeul Day.

...HE FOUND THE CORPORATE WORLD TOO RESTRICTIVE FOR HIS ARTISTIC TEMPERAMENT...

Linguists say that Hangeul is the simplest writing system in the world and can be learned in just a few hours. However, in the 1980s, it was clear to Ahn that the typographical representation of Hangeul needed modernizing.

Existing Hangeul typefaces were dull-looking, rigidly square, and monospaced. In response, in 1985, he designed the Ahn Sang-soo typeface with a non-square design that was fully proportional. He was inspired by German typographer Jan Tschichold's 1928 book *Die Neue Typographie* (*The New Typography*).

Because these new characters did not have to fit the full width of a square, components could be reused instead of adjusting and distorting them into the available space. This was a revolutionary move: non-square soon became a new typographical classification, unique to Korean, and more designers started to design non-square fonts.

In 1988 Ahn received an award from the Korean Language Society for contributions to Hangeul design. And his innovation ultimately enabled Hangeul to evolve into a functional medium for today's digital world.

Opposite: Poster by Peter Ridley using the Ahn Sang-soo typeface

been featured in over 40 shows. He regularly travels abroad to lecture on his projects and promote Asian design developments and ideas. He has published several design books, essays, and papers, and translated seminal works by designers Jan Tschichold and Emil Ruder into Korean.

Since 1988 Ahn has been the editor and art director of underground art-culture magazine *bogoseo/ bogoseo* (report/report). And in 1991 he began his professorship in typography at Hongik University, his alma mater, which he pursued until 2012.

In 2013 he established an experimental design school, PaTI (Paju Typography Institute) in Paju Bookcity, where he continues to develop Korean typography in partnership with generations of designers. He told Korean online magazine *Kocis*, "I don't simply teach. I share what I have learned and that in which I am most confident. After all, schools are not meant to be private possessions. I will continue to devote myself to collaborative creations."

Internationally, Ahn was vice-president from

"LETTERS ARE KEY TO HOW MUCH OF A CULTURE CAN BE PRESERVED, AND HOW MUCH IT WILL SHINE IN HISTORY."

Ahn Sang-soo

Ahn himself recognizes the historic importance of this work. "Letters are the key to how much of a culture can be preserved, and how much it will shine in history," he said. "The same goes for Hangeul. If Hangeul had not been invented, would Korea even exist? Korean culture maybe would not have developed."

His list of other design achievements, both in Korea and abroad, is expansive. Major projects include a new design system for the Korean Buddhist Chogye Order (2004), the *Ssamzie Art Book* (1997), the Life-peace movement symbol (2004), and a series of cultural posters.

Ahn has also led the design and production of many major international exhibitions, and his own work has

1997 to 2001 of Icograda (International Council of Graphic Design Associations) and was chairman of the Icograda Millennium Oullim Congress 2000 as well as TypoJanchi 2001, an international typography event held in Seoul.

Ahn isn't just interested in typography; he has pursued a number of creative projects. For example, in 1988 he took a self-portrait in which he covered one eye. He was fascinated by this image and launched a photography portrait project—the *One Eye Exhibition*—featuring over 30,000 pictures of people doing the same pose. Images from the project, from 2004 to the present, can be found on ssahn.com.

AHN SANG-SOO

SUSAN KARE

HER DESIGNS ARE SO SIMPLE AND BRILLIANT THAT YOU MIGHT OVERLOOK THEM.

AMERICAN
B. 1954

HIGHLIGHTS
Icons, fonts

CHARACTERISTICS
Playful, concise, functional

Opposite: The Command key on a Macintosh operating system

If you use an Apple computer, there's one designer whose work you've probably spent more of your life staring at than any other, yet you may not even know her name. Susan Kare created the most iconic graphic elements of the Macintosh operating system, including the Trash can, the Command key, the Lasso, the Pan hand, the Pouring Paint can, the Happy Mac, Sad Mac, and more. And in doing so, she influenced generations of designers working in icon design and beyond.

Kare was born in 1954 in Ithaca, New York, where her parents studied at Cornell University. Her father was later a professor at the University of Pennsylvania and Director of the Monell Chemical Senses Center, a research facility for sensory physiology. Her brother was aerospace engineer Jordin Kare, and her mother, a librarian, taught Susan needlepoint and cross-stitch embroidery and encouraged her interest in drawing, painting, and crafts.

Kare originally hoped to work as either a fine artist or a teacher, so she earned a BA in art at Mount Holyoke College in 1975, then an MA and a Ph.D. in Fine Arts at New York University in 1978.

She moved to San Francisco to work at the Fine Arts Museums of San Francisco on a Rockefeller Fellowship. In 1982, she received a call from Andy Hertzfeld, a high school friend from Philadelphia, who was an early Apple employee. He asked her to sketch a few icons and font elements as sample graphics for the Macintosh computer in development, in exchange for an Apple II.

Kare had no formal experience in computer graphics or typeface design, but she drew on her knowledge

of mosaics, needlepoint, and other "digital" art. She mocked up icons using graph paper she bought at University Art, a landmark art-and-design store in Palo Alto.

Kare was subsequently invited to join Apple as the "Macintosh artist", and she was the only graphic designer in the Mac software group. Her primary objective, she was told, was to help make a computer for non-technical people, a computer "for the rest of us".

Her monochrome icons needed to fit within small (16 x 16 and 32 × 32) pixel grids, but she still astonished the team with the personality she injected into them.

Alternately, her cloverleaf symbol for the Command key was inspired by the Saint Hannes cross, a road sign image seen in Nordic countries to indicate a place of interest.

Influence doesn't necessarily mean copying, though. "I don't use work from the past as a literal guide," she told *Cosmopolitan* in 2016. "Rather, those artifacts reinforce a view that simple images can communicate with wide audiences over time. Icon design is like solving a puzzle, trying to marry an image and idea that, ideally, will be easy for people to understand and remember."

> "ICON DESIGN IS LIKE SOLVING A PUZZLE, TRYING TO MARRY AN IMAGE AND IDEA THAT, IDEALLY, WILL BE EASY FOR PEOPLE TO UNDERSTAND AND REMEMBER."
>
> Susan Kare

Left: The startup Happy Mac icon that greeted Mac computer users in the 1980s

Below: Some more icons from an early Mac control panel

The sense of fun Kare brought to her work was the icing on the cake, but not the cake itself. She believes that, overall, icons should function like road signs, and be clear, concise, and memorable. She's been said to remark that no-one is clamouring to redesign or upgrade the stop sign.

Kare spent a year refining the core visual design language of the original Macintosh, which was introduced in 1984. This included illustrations for marketing materials as well as typefaces, icons, and other user interface graphics such as the control panel. Some icons, such as the Lasso, the Pan hand, the Pouring paint can, and the Document (a page with a folded corner), became universal staples of computing across multiple platforms. Others, including the Happy Mac icon that appeared on startup, the Command key symbol, and the wristwatch cursor, remain distinctly Apple to this day.

These friendly icons, along with the Macintosh's visual interface—which for the first time allowed people to move things around on screen with a mouse—helped erode prevailing stereotypes that computers were cold, intimidating, and overly complicated. With the Macintosh a cultural shift took place, which meant that people were far less intimidated about owning and using a computer at home.

Kare also designed the first proportionally spaced digital font families, including Chicago, New York, Geneva, the monospaced Monaco, the "emoji" font Cairo, and the ransom-note style San Francisco. Chicago was part of Apple's brand identity until 1997, and was used in four generations of the Apple iPod. She produced other early fonts for the Macintosh, which were named after train stops on Philadelphia's Main Line, including Overbrook, Merion, Ardmore, Rosemont, and Paoli.

In 1986 Kare followed Apple founder Steve Jobs in leaving the company to launch NeXT; she became its tenth employee and creative director. She introduced Jobs to her design hero, Paul Rand (see Chapter 16), and hired Rand to design NeXT's logo, brand identity, and launch materials. Kare later became an independent designer; her clients included Microsoft, IBM, Facebook, General Magic, and Intel. She created

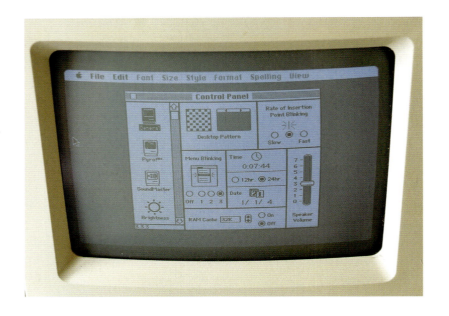

"THERE IS A LOT OF VERY GOOD 'PIXEL' DESIGN WORK BEFORE THE 20TH CENTURY."

Susan Kare

the designs for Windows Solitaire and icons and other graphic elements for Windows 3.0.

Kare became a founding partner of Susan Kare LLP in 1989. In 2003, after a recommendation from U.S. Representative Nancy Pelosi, she was appointed to the Citizens Coinage Advisory Committee for the United States Mint. Between 2006 and 2010 she produced hundreds of 64 × 64 pixel icons for the virtual gifts feature of Facebook. Initially, profits from gift sales were donated to Susan G. Komen for the Cure, a breast-cancer charity.

In 2015 Kare was hired by Pinterest as a product design lead, and in 2021 became a design architect at Niantic Labs, the augmented reality development company well-known for Pokémon Go. She's been designing limited edition icon prints since 2011 at kareprints.com, and designs home goods for Areaware.

While Kare may be famous for her digital designs, she sees the medium itself as not the most important factor. In 2018 she told the creativity blog Lenny, 'When you study art history, you learn that there is very little that is completely new, and in many ways digital art is no different. I love to derive inspiration from all types of images: mosaics, hieroglyphics, petroglyphs, woven patterns in textiles, and needlework. There is a lot of very good 'pixel' design work before the 20th century, such as a 1760 sampler by Elizabeth Laidman that looks like a bitmap font."

Below: Susan hand painting a woodcut in her design studio

ART SIMS

"WHEN OPPORTUNITY SHOWS UP, EITHER YOU'RE READY OR YOU'RE NOT. I WAS READY."

AMERICAN
B. 1954

HIGHLIGHTS
Movie posters, album covers

CHARACTERISTICS
Hip-hop aesthetic,
bold colours,
expressive typography

Opposite: Sims's design for Spike Lee's Clockers film

The movie poster is one of those graphic-design tasks that looks easy but is devilishly difficult to master. The best in the genre become almost as iconic as the movies themselves—sometimes even more so—because they sum up a moment in time and the feelings evoked by the movie in a single, simple composition. No wonder they are so collectible. And Art Sims is among the greatest practitioners of this rare art.

Sims was born in Detroit, Michigan, in 1954. He won awards for his artwork in elementary school, and his mother—a grade-school teacher—nurtured his creativity, guiding him through school and instilling a love of learning. He attended Cass Technical High School in Detroit then won a full scholarship to Michigan State University from 1971 to 1975. One of his teachers there told him he'd never make it. But rather than be defeated, Sims decided to double down and prove the teacher wrong.

While still in college, he landed a summer job as an art director at Columbia Records in Los Angeles, where he designed album covers including *That's How Much I Love You* by the Manhattans, and *Atma* by Michal Urbaniak's Fusion. After graduating, he worked as an art director at EMI. During this period, he produced a series of album covers including Little River Band's eponymous debut, *French Kiss* by Bob Welch, *Minnie* by Minnie Riperton, and *Shine* by Average White Band. Eventually he was fired by EMI, which did not like the fact that he had done freelance work outside his main job.

In 1981 Sims launched his own company, 11:24 Design Advertising. The name refers to a verse in the Book of Mark: "Therefore I tell you, whatever you ask for in prayer, believe that you have received it, and it will be yours." A contact in Sims's office connected him to Steven Spielberg's project *The Color Purple*, an epic tale spanning 40 years in the life of an African-American woman living in the south (played by Whoopi Goldberg), who survives abuse and bigotry. "When opportunity shows up, either you're ready or you're not. I was ready," he told the American Institute of Graphic Arts. "I rose to the occasion. I put my most creative thoughts in my mind and came up with the most beautiful images I could come up with. I wasn't taking any prisoners with this one. I was out to show how good I was."

In 1986 he saw *She's Gotta Have It*, Spike Lee's groundbreaking romantic comedy about a woman and her three lovers. Inspired by the movie, he sought out the director and was commissioned to create the poster for his second film, *School Daze*, set at a historically black college. It was the start of a long relationship, which heightened after Lee heard that Sims's poster for his film *New Jack City* (1991), featuring Wesley Snipes, was so popular that people were vandalizing bus shelters to steal it.

Sims's posters for Lee's films weren't just great designs; they were also groundbreaking for bringing the hip-hop aesthetic outside of album covers and into the mainstream of graphic design.

Sims had two broad approaches. The first was typified by his poster for *Do the Right Thing* (1989), which featured a saturated colour palette that evoked the lighthearted pop-music videos of the era.

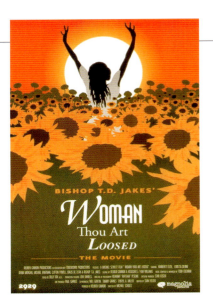

Left: *Woman Thou Art Loosed* film poster, 2004

Opposite: The strikingly simple but profoundly affecting trailer poster for *Malcolm X*, 1992

The second can be seen in the poster for *Malcolm X* (1992), starring Denzel Washington, which swapped star power for typography. Featuring little more than a white slab-serif X against a solid black background, it visually echoed the stark record covers of political rappers Public Enemy. According to the cultural blog *A Rabbit's Foot*, Sims asked Washington, "'Do we do the young Malcolm… the old Malcolm… the angry Malcolm… or the Malcolm before he passed away?' Washington responded, 'Look, man, he's so complicated. I don't know… Let's just do the X!'"

Another landmark poster design was for 1990's *Mo' Better Blues*, which follows an ambitious jazz musician of debatable morals, also played by Denzel Washington. A poster within the poster covers up a poster for Lee's previous movie, *Do the Right Thing*, symbolically posing the question of whether the main character in this movie does the right thing.

His most controversial work to date is his poster for Lee's 2000 satirical comedy *Bamboozled*. The design sparked the attention of the Nation of Islam, the black nationalist organization once led by Malcolm X. The group initially planned to boycott Lee's film because they felt the poster played on crass racial stereotypes. However, when they learned that Sims himself was African-American, they ended their protest.

Sims has continued to prioritize work by and centred around African-Americans, including designs for the superhero movie *Black Panther*. Other memorable movie-poster designs include *Clockers* (1995), *Dreamgirls* (2006), *Jungle Fever* (1991), *Summer of Sam* (1999), *Love & Basketball* (2000), *Crooklyn* (1994), and *Brooklyn's Finest* (2009).

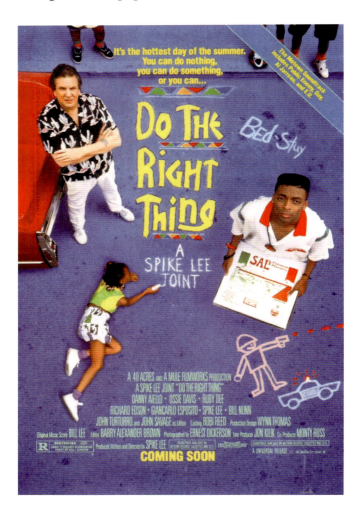

Above: The *Do The Right Thing* film poster, subsequently papered over in the poster for *Mo' Better Blues*

NAOTO FUKASAWA

HIS WORLD RENOWNED PRODUCT AND FURNITURE DESIGNS SIT EASILY IN SPACES.

You wouldn't describe Naoto Fukasawa as having a unique style. In fact, his overall design philosophy is to turn that concept on its head and remove any style or branding from his objects, as a point of principle.

"Design means observing objectively," he told the blog Designboom in 2004. "It means being aware of our living nature, a simple element in the larger environment. I like when a project doesn't sell my name or my characteristics, when it is just an object that happens to be there, …no, not anonymous, just natural."

JAPANESE
B. 1956

HIGHLIGHTS
Product design, furniture design

CHARACTERISTICS
Neutral, functional, non-branded

Above: Chair design on display at the Vitra Design Museum

Born in Kōfu, Yamanashi Prefecture, Japan in 1956, Fukasawa studied product design at Tama Art University in Tokyo, graduating in 1980. After graduating he worked as a product developer at Seiko Epson, where he designed products such as wrist TVs and mini printers using micro-technology.

In 1988 he joined design firm ID Two, a predecessor to design consulting firm IDEO in San Francisco.

There, he worked on a number of products related to Silicon Valley's computing and electronics industry. He was also involved in the development of a design language and design concept for Apple.

In 1996 Fukasawa returned to Japan to start and head up IDEO's Tokyo office, acting as a design consultant to many major Japanese companies. In 1999 he came up with the idea of a wall-mounted CD player that was released by Muji and became popular worldwide. Its design is based on an off-white, rounded square with the laser apparatus exposed, and the speakers located in the lower two corners behind a plastic grille. He wrote that it was inspired by ventilation fans with blades that turn when a cord is pulled, with the wind noise eventually balancing out into a constant flow.

Above: A display of wall-mounted lights shown at Vitra Campus, Rhein, Germany

Right: Japanese model Moga Mogami displays KDDI's new stylish mobile phone INOFOFAR XV at launch event in Tokyo, 2018

In 2003 he launched his own company, Naoto Fukasawa Design. One of his early projects was the Infobar mobile phone, which became a design leader in Japan. A slab with candy-bar keys and a touchscreen, it reconceptualized the phone as a portable computer long before the appearance of the iPhone, and at a time when phones were still primarily used for making calls.

He has worked with several Italian furniture companies including B&B Italia, Driade, Magis, Artemide, Danese, and Boffi as well as companies in Germany and northern Europe. Since 2001, when he became a consultant for Muji, his primary focus has been the design of household products and electronic devices. His minimalist, objective approach highlights the functionality of his products without sacrificing character.

In 2006 Fukasawa curated an exhibition with English furniture designer Jasper Morrison titled Super Normal. It was inspired by the observation that objects which appear ordinary and unremarkable are often the easiest for people to use in practice. As Fukasawa later explained in a video for the Louisiana Museum of Modern Art in Denmark in 2022, he believes the best-designed products needn't be noticeable. "They just have to be there when you need them, without causing trouble. They show their love best by being quiet."

Super Normal presented 200 objects ranging from the Bialetti espresso maker to anonymous, mass-produced objects such as disposable plastic plates. The same design concept can be seen in Fukasawa's work with Muji, where products are created with an anti-branding approach, not presenting any traits that characterize the object.

Since 2014 Fukasawa has taught Integrated Design at Tama Art University as a professor and is now its vice president. He has also previously taught at Musashino Art University in western Tokyo. Since 2012, he is the director of The Nihon Mingei-kan (The Japan Folk Crafts Museum) and, in 2022, he founded the Design Science Foundation.

His design philosophy is based on the idea of "design dissolving in behaviour." This approach relies on observing how people act and react in their everyday lives, and finding solutions that link the design to those behaviours.

In his 2018 monograph, Fukasawa describes design as "attributing countenance to an object," and he is known for coining the phrase "without thought" by way of explaining how design can respond to people's unconscious impulses. In other words, objects should not be judged when seen for the first time, because their initial essence will only be realized when they are actually used.

In his latest project, before this book went to press, Fukasawa created a minimalist design for SodaStream's latest carbonator, the enso.

NAOTO FUKASAWA

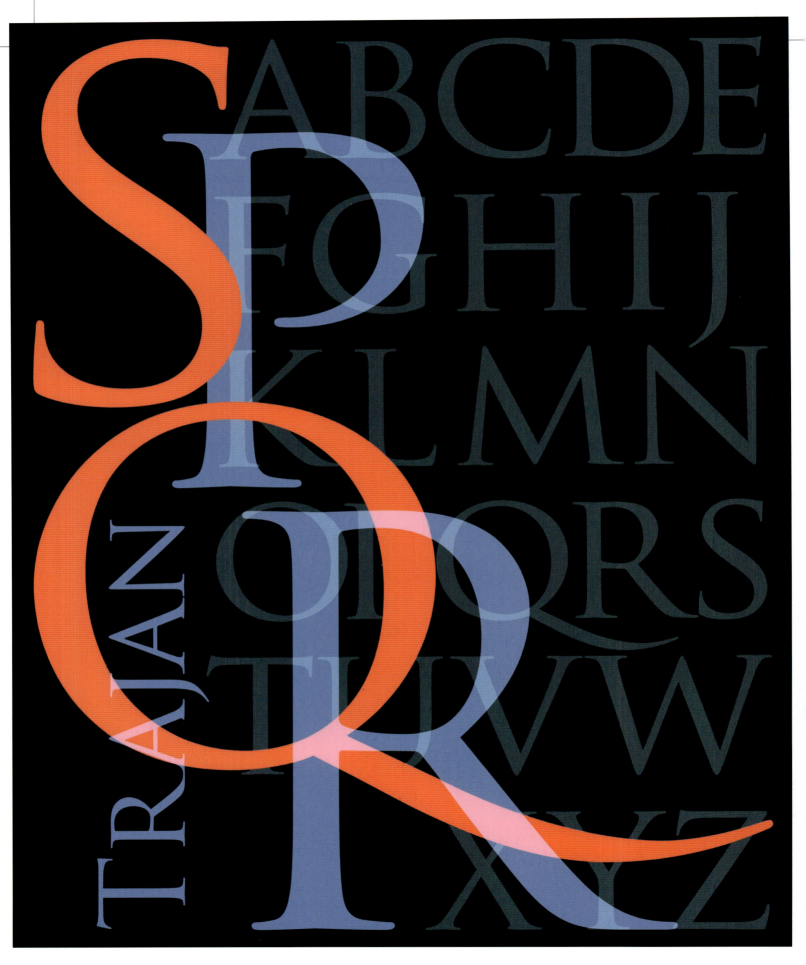

CAROL
TWOMBLY

HER CONTRIBUTION TO DIGITAL TYPOGRAPHY IS IMMEASURABLE SINCE SHE IS BEHIND THE FONTS THAT WE SEE DAILY OUT IN THE WORLD.

AMERICAN
B. 1959

HIGHLIGHTS
Type design

CHARACTERISTICS
Digital fonts based on ancient lettering

Opposite: Poster art by Peter Ridley showcasing Trajan, one of several fonts designed by Twombly

Type design seems so invisible to many people that its impact on our society is often downplayed, or even ignored. But in an era when almost every piece of communication is digital, its importance cannot be overstated. In turn, to not include Carol Twombly on our list would have been inconceivable, as her contribution to digital typography has been immense.

She was born in 1959, in Concord, Massachusetts. During her childhood in New England, she explored a variety of artistic disciplines.

She followed her brother, who was studying architecture, to the Rhode Island School of Design, where she initially studied sculpture. Eventually, though, Twombly switched her major to graphic design. She recalled: "I discovered that communicating through graphics—by placing black shapes on a white page—offered a welcome balance between freedom and structure." She credits her graphic-design professors, Charles Bigelow and Kris Holmes, and visiting instructor Gerard Unger, for getting her interested in typography.

… A WELCOME BALANCE BETWEEN FREEDOM AND STRUCTURE…

After graduating, she spent a year working in a Boston graphic-design studio called Bigelow & Holmes before accepting an invitation to join a small group of students in a newly formed digital typography program at Stanford University. She was one of only five people to graduate from the course, which lasted just two years.

This was a time before drawing apps, so Twombly created lettering by editing numerically on an early digital type-design system. To create the initial designs, she would outline letters on vellum, ink them in, and then tack them to a wall, where they could be viewed through a reducing glass.

She worked for the studio for the next four years. In 1984 she entered her first original type design—a collaboration with Robert Slimbach—in a global competition sponsored by Morisawa, a Japanese manufacturer of typesetting equipment.

The design won first prize in the Latin text category, and the company subsequently licensed and marketed her design under the name Mirarae.

Above: Victor McLindon's portrait of Carol Twombly

Right: Poster art by Peter Ridley featuring Twombly's Zebrawood font

In 1988 she joined Adobe as a designer. During her 11 years with the software giant, she designed several highly popular text and display typefaces. Her first was the serif typeface Trajan. The design is based on the letterforms of capitalis monumentalis (Roman square capitals) used on the base of Trajan's Column in Rome. It was designed for display instead of printed text, specifically for use in large sizes. Twombly developed the design by taking a full-size rubbing of the inscription. Trajan is an all-capitals typeface—the Romans did not use lower-case letters—and it has appeared on hundreds of film posters, from Shakespearean dramas such as Titus (1999) to horrors like The Human Centipede (2009).

Her next project, that same year, was to translate Carolingian versals (decorative capital letters) into a digital typeface called Charlemagne. Her source was a page from the Anglo-Saxon Benedictional of Saint Æthelwold in the British Library. Also in 1989 came the font Lithos, inspired by ancient Greek inscriptions. Adobe marketed the three fonts as Modern Ancients.

In 1990 she created Adobe Caslon, a digital evolution of an 18th-century typeface designed by William Caslon. Based on Caslon's specimen pages, printed between 1734 and 1770, the new version added features that are now considered standard in high-quality digital fonts, including small caps, old-style figures, swash letters, ligatures, alternate letters, fractions, subscripts and superscripts, and matching ornaments. The font has been used for body text in The New Yorker and is one of the two official typefaces of the University of Virginia and the University of Southern California.

In 1994 Twombly released Nueva, an original design, and in 1997 came Chaparral. The latter took inspiration from 19th-century slab-serif forms and 16th-century Roman book hand (a calligraphic form), and was designed in collaboration with calligrapher Linnea Lundquist.

Under Twombly's art direction, fonts such as Ponderosa, Pepperwood, Zebrawood, and Rosewood were developed at Adobe as part of a project to revive American display typefaces in wood type from the 1880s. In 1994 she was awarded the Prix Charles Peignot, given by the Association Typographique Internationale. She was the first woman, and only the second American, to receive this honour.

However, Twombly was uncomfortable being in the public eye at conferences and in Adobe marketing materials. She also grew dissatisfied with changes at Adobe and with her changing role at the company.

> "THE CHALLENGE OF COMMUNICATING AN IDEA OR FEELING WITHIN THE FURTHER CONFINES OF THE LATIN ALPHABET LED ME FROM GRAPHIC DESIGN INTO TYPE DESIGN."

In 1999 she left both Adobe and her career in type design to pursue other artistic interests.

She has continued to explore non-computer-based arts, including weaving, natural-object sculpture, silk painting, and making shekeres (hand-held African percussion instruments) with which to accompany her fellow conga players.

CAROL TWOMBLY

KARIM RASHID

"I DESIGN EVERYTHING EXCEPT GUNS OR ANYTHING RELATED TO WAR OR VIOLENCE."

Having worked in over 40 countries and created more than 4,000 produced designs, Karim Rashid has become a leading figure in the fields of product design, interior design, fashion, furniture, and lighting design. And he's not just prolific; his mission to change the world through design has been influential on designers everywhere.

Rashid was born in 1960 in Cairo, to an English mother and an Egyptian father. He was born with the umbilical cord wrapped around his neck and had developmental delays, which meant that he was unable to speak until he was four. His family emigrated to Mississauga, Ontario, Canada when he was five, and he recalls sketching the luggage he saw on the ship to Canada.

His father was a painter and set designer for television and film; he also designed furniture and dresses for Rashid's mother. In 2019 Rashid told the online publication *Autodesk*, "He was a Renaissance man, and on the coffee table, he would always have books from the library—fashion designers like Yves Saint Laurent and Pierre Cardin; industrial designers like Raymond Loewy and Philippe Starck; architects like Oscar Niemeyer, Le Corbusier, and Michael Graves; artists like Picasso and Warhol."

Rashid's love of bright colours started at an early age. When he was 12, he painted his bedroom yellow and orange. Later, for his high-school graduation, he dyed his hair and nails pink and fashioned himself a pink satin suit—he's still known for wearing pink. His determination to enter the design world heightened at 18 when he visited the International Furniture Fair in Milan for the first time and became fascinated by the work of Italian architect and designer Achille Castiglioni.

From 1978 to 1982 Rashid attended Carleton University in Canada, where he received a Bachelor of Industrial Design, with honours. He then went to Naples, where he studied industrial and product design from 1982 to 1983 under the tutelage of Castiglioni as well as Ettore Sottsass and Gaetano Pesce.

EGYPTIAN
B. 1960

HIGHLIGHTS
Product design, interior design, fashion design, furniture design, lighting design

CHARACTERISTICS
Flowing lines, vivid colours, sensual shapes

Left and below: Globalove chairs and below Karim's sketches for the chairs

Once his studies were complete, he moved to Milan and spent a year working at Rodolfo Bonetto Studio, the eponymous firm of the famous jazz drummer-turned-designer. Starting in 1984 Rashid spent seven years working for KAN Industrial Designers in Canada before opening a design studio in New York in 1993.

Some of the earliest products he designed were business phones for Canadian telecoms firm Mitel, television sets for Brionvega, and dashboards for Fiat. All of these designs were made from plastic, which aligned perfectly with his vision of democratic design: beautiful products that everyone, not just the elite, could enjoy.

Over the course of his career, Rashid has developed a number of products that are now considered

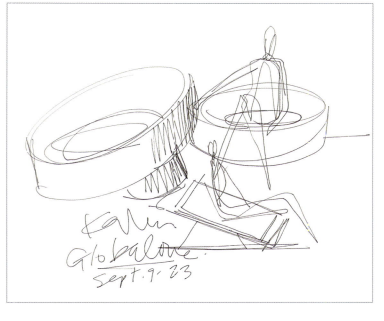

icons of democratic design. These include the translucent Garbo waste bin, designed for Canadian plastics company Umbra in 1994, which can be used variously as a clothes hamper, vase, and Champagne cooler. It's constructed from a highly tactile polypropylene material, and the design explores ideas of dematerialization. "You feel in a sense that there is very little there," Rashid said, "yet it is so flexible that basically it's indestructible."

In 1999, Rashid was inspired to design a plastic chair that would be comfortable, attractive and durable. The result was the Oh chair, created for Umbra. It earned him the 1999 IDEA Award and since 2000 it has been part of the permanent collection of the San Francisco Museum of Modern Art.

Alongside mass-market products for Umbra, Bobble, and 3M, Rashid is known for designing luxury goods for Christofle, Veuve Clicquot, and Alessi; furniture for Bonaldo and Vondom; and lighting for Artemide and FontanaArte. He has collaborated with Asus and Samsung on tech products, and designed

Left: Shower room in 9 Hanover Street, London W1

Above: The Kairo collection, made from marble, for Luce di Carrara

Left: 9 Hanover Street, the luxury residential development in W1 London

lighting for Artemide, Swarovski, and Martinelli Luce; furniture for Magister and Bonaldo; cars for Audi and Hyundai; and packaging for Issey Miyake and Hugo Boss.

Interiors and hotel designs are another speciality, including the Morimoto restaurant in Philadelphia, Semiramis Hotel in Athens, the University of Naples Metro Station, Nhow Hotel in Berlin, Matisse Beach Club in Australia, MyBrickell in Miami, and Amoje Food Capital in South Korea. In 1999 he was commissioned to design manhole covers for the sewers of New York City. On his Facebook page he states, "I design everything except guns or anything related to war or violence."

Functionality and minimalism are key to his work, and he was dubbed the "Prince of Plastic" by Time magazine. However, Rashid also wants to make people feel at ease and make an emotional connection, an approach he calls "sensual minimalism." He outlined his philosophy in his Karimanifesto: "I believe that we could be living in an entirely different world—one that is full of real contemporary inspiring objects, spaces, places, worlds, spirits, and experiences… My real desire is to see people live in the modus of our time, to participate in the contemporary world, and to release themselves from nostalgia, antiquated traditions, old rituals, kitsch, and the meaningless. We should be conscious and attune with this world in this moment. If human nature is to live in the past—to change the world is to change human nature."

Above: ATLAS Max high-end collectible for HOMMI, with a limited numbered and stamped release of 1000

Rashid is a frequent guest lecturer at universities and conferences, and has published a number of books. His 2015 monograph XX features 400 pages of work selected from the previous 20 years. He has won more than 300 awards and is a perennial winner of the Red Dot Award, Good Design award, Pentawards, and IDSA Industrial Design Excellence award.

He has received honorary doctorates from OCAD University (2006), the Pratt Institute (2004), Corcoran College of Art & Design (2005), Carleton University (2016), and the British Institute of Interior Design. His work is in the permanent collections of more than 20 museums and galleries worldwide.

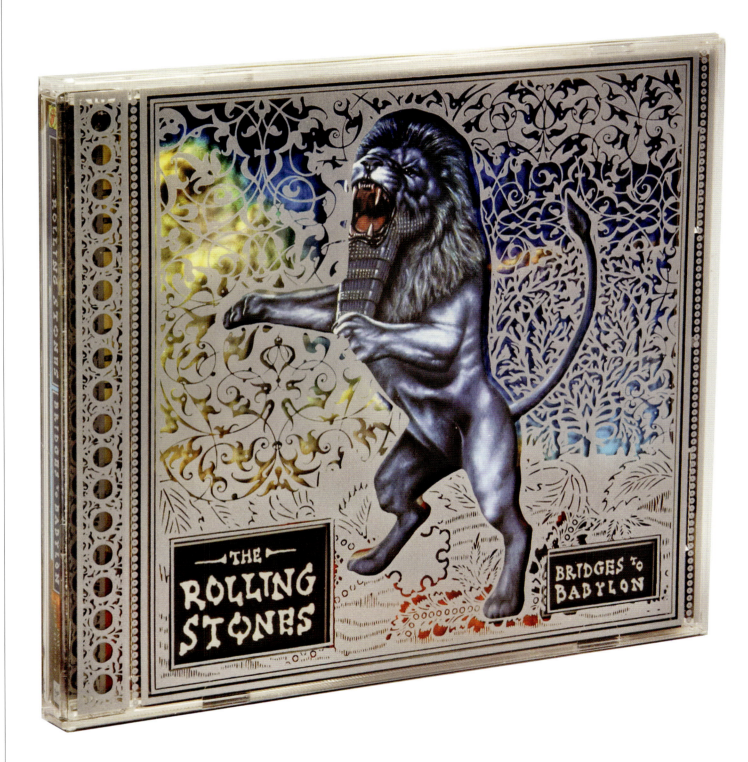

STEFAN SAGMEISTER

IF YOU ASK ANYONE WORKING IN GRAPHIC DESIGN TO LIST THEIR HEROES, THERE'S A HIGH CHANCE THAT STEFAN SAGMEISTER WILL BE MENTIONED.

AUSTRIAN
B. 1962

HIGHLIGHTS
Graphic design, record covers, branding

CHARACTERISTICS
Handmade typography, punk influences, themes of nudity and sexuality

Opposite: Sagmeister's design for the Rolling Stones' Bridges to Babylon album cover

More than any contemporary design legend, Stefan Sagmeister evokes the air of the rock star. And that's not just because he's designed a number of iconic record covers. More broadly, whatever project he's working on, the end result will instantly convey his deep-seated unwillingness to conform to "acceptable norms."

Sagmeister was born in 1962 in Bregenz, Austria. He began his design career at the age of 15, working on a left-wing youth magazine called *Alphorn*. He made his first foray into DIY graphics for its Anarchy issue, when he got his fellow pupils to lie down on the playground in the shape of the letter A and took a photo of them from the school roof.

After leaving high school, Sagmeister enrolled in an engineering college, but changed his mind and went to study graphic design at the Hochschule für Angewandte Kunst (University of Applied Arts) in Vienna. He was initially rejected due to his poor drawing skills, but succeeded on the second attempt. After graduating in 1986 he received a Fulbright scholarship to study at the Pratt Institute in New York, where he received a Master of Fine Arts degree. After three years in the US, Sagmeister returned to Austria to complete his mandatory military service. He opted to perform community service for refugee centres, and then stayed in Austria to work as a graphic designer.

In 1991 he moved to Hong Kong, where he worked as a typographer for an ad agency, Leo Burnett's Hong Kong Design Group. While there, he created controversy with his poster for the 4As advertising awards ceremony, featuring a painting in traditional Cantonese style with four men showing their behinds. A number of agencies boycotted the ceremony in protest at this lewdness.

In 1993 Sagmeister returned to New York to work at Tibor Kalman's design company M&Co., which sponsored his green card. However, in the same year, Kalman decided to close the studio to focus on editing Colors magazine for the Benetton Group in Rome. It was the spur Sagmeister needed to set up his own studio, Sagmeister Inc. Continuing his fascination with nudity, the designer sent out a nude photo of himself to publicize the new company.

Sagmeister was primarily interested in working on music designs, and his first cover artwork was for an Austrian friend's underground band. His design

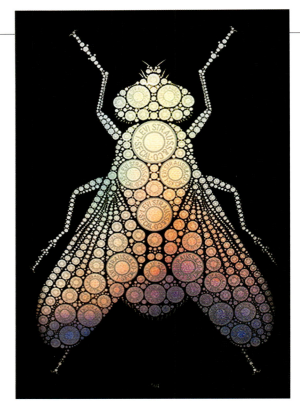

Above: Poster advertising the Levi Strauss 501 jeans, which had a button fly hence this 'button fly'

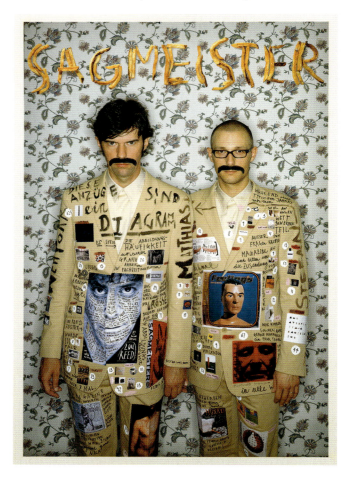

Above: Stefan Sagmeister and Matthias Ernstberger wearing suits that show their work sized by how often it is mentioned in the press

for H.P. Zinker's *Mountains of Madness* grabbed attention by using an optical illusion. By placing the CD cover inside a red plastic case, what looked like a calm old man became angry when the booklet was removed from the case. He used the same strategy later for his book *Made You Look*. The CD cover design was nominated for a Grammy; Lou Reed came to the studio because he had seen it, and this put Sagmeister on the map as a designer for music.

Sagmeister went on to be a long-standing collaborator with artists including Reed, David Byrne, Brian Eno, and the Rolling Stones. The studio also created graphics, branding, and packaging for a long list of clients including HBO, the Guggenheim Museum, Time Warner, Levi's, Adobe, Red Bull, BMW, NYC, the Olympic committee, the Museum of Modern Art, the American Institute of Graphic Arts (AIGA), Random House, Seed magazine, and *The New York Times*. Alumni include the celebrated designers Martin Woodtli, Hjalti Karlsson, and Jan Wilker.

Sagmeister's work has no specific "look," and that's no accident. He has often decried bland and boring branding, and is constantly looking for inventive and original ways to approach design, including a variety of materials and techniques. However, it's possible to identify some common characteristics in much of his extensive portfolio.

One is an interest in grungy, handcrafted lettering as a way of offsetting and challenging the sameness of digital typography. Another is a willingness to use nonconformist and shocking imagery, typically focused on nudity and sexuality, which stands out in an era dominated by cancel culture and self-censorship. More broadly, he has arguably translated the spirit of anarchist graphics, punk album art, and fanzines from the 1970s better than anyone into the world of modern design.

All of these elements can be seen in one of his most famous posters, to publicize an AIGA lecture at Cranbrook Academy of Art, near Detroit. Sagmeister stripped naked and asked an intern to carve the entire text of his talk onto his torso with an X-Acto knife, then photographed the result. The idea was to visually convey the pain that accompanies most design projects.

Above: Part of the exhibition *Seoul, Now is Better* at the Dongdaemun Design Plaza, Seoul, South Korea

In 2010 a 23-year-old American designer called Jessica Walsh, who had spent 10 months working at Pentagram and was working as the art director of *Print* magazine, wrote to Sagmeister seeking career guidance. Sagmeister was impressed by her portfolio and offered her a job. Two years later they became partners, and the studio became Sagmeister & Walsh.

This partnership was ideal because Walsh took over the client aspect of the business, allowing Sagmeister to travel more and focus on his films. Continuing the Sagmeister tradition, the new partners released a photo of themselves naked in their office to announce the renaming of the firm. It lasted until 2019, when Walsh left to found her own studio, &Walsh.

Sagmeister has been hugely influential on the profession, not just for his work but for the philosophies that surround it. For example, he famously takes a year-long sabbatical approximately every seven years; he spends the year experimenting with personal work and refreshing himself as a designer. He explains this approach, and encourages others to pursue it, in his 2009 TED talk "The Power of Time Off."

In 2023 he pushed back against conventional thinking once more by releasing *Why Now Is Better*. In the face of contemporary narratives that suggest things have never been worse, it uses both historical art and data visualization to highlight just how much life has improved for the majority of people.

Sagmeister's work has been exhibited all over the world, and he has received a number of awards. These include Grammys for the Talking Heads box set *Once in a Lifetime* (2005) and the David Byrne and Brian Eno album *Everything That Happens Will Happen Today* (2010); the National Design Award for Communications from Cooper Hewitt, Smithsonian Design Museum (2005); and the Golden Medal of Honor of the Republic of Austria (2013). In 2018, he was voted Austrian of the Year by Austrian newspaper *Die Presse* (2018).

Below: ily espresso cup showing its reflective surface

171

GAIL ANDERSON

"I'M ALL ABOUT COMMUNICATION THROUGH DESIGN."

AMERICAN
B. 1962

HIGHLIGHTS
Editorial design, poster design, stamp design

CHARACTERISTICS
Innovation in typography, sense of fun

Opposite: A poster design for New York's The School of Visual Arts

Born in the Bronx, New York in 1962, to a family of Jamaican immigrants, Gail Anderson's love of art began at an early age. She recalls a teacher reacting with surprise when at five years old, she started drawing her classmates in profile.

As a teen, she enjoyed making Elton John posters, copying her parents' album covers, and crafting her own magazines based on the Jackson 5 and The Partridge Family. She created the latter by physically pasting together newspaper and magazine cuttings with her own drawings and text; even including kissable centrefolds.

"I knew that I liked laying things out," she said in an interview with AEF in 2019. "I liked to draw, but I knew that it was putting the pieces together [...] there was something really fun about that."

Above: Poster art for Man of La Mancha

Gradually, she began to look into what was then called "commercial art" as a career. Motivated by an enthusiastic art teacher at high school, Miss Francis, Anderson read books about art, entered competitions, worked on the school magazine and yearbook, and took Saturday art classes at Pratt Manhattan. She was also encouraged by a cousin who worked at CBS Records as an art director.

She went on to attend the School of Visual Arts in New York City, becoming the first in her family to get a college education. There, she was taught by a number of influential women designers including Paula Scher (see chapter 33), Carin Goldberg and Louise Fili. After graduating in 1984 with a BFA, Scher helped her secure a job as an assistant designer at Vintage Books, an imprint of Penguin Random House.

Anderson then spent two years at The Boston Globe Sunday Magazine (1985-87), where her boss Lynn Stanley became a big influence on her career and helped her mature as a designer. She then moved to Rolling Stone magazine from 1987-2002, starting as designer and deputy art director before rising to become senior art director, under the direction of Fred Woodward.

From 2002-2010, Anderson made a move from editorial to advertising design, after becoming the creative director at SpotCo, a New York agency specialising in advertising for the arts and entertainment. During this period, she oversaw a team of designers that worked on Broadway shows such as Avenue Q, Ragtime and La Cage aux Folles.

Her ability to capture the essence of complex narratives in compelling visual form—as seen in posters for productions including George C. Wolfe's musical Harlem Song and August Wilson's Gem of the Ocean—played a crucial role in shaping the visual identity of American theatre for the modern era.

In 2012, she launched her own studio with her creative partner Joe Newton called AND (Anderson Newton Design). A creative agency dedicated to sophisticated yet playful design, with a focus on typography, its long client list includes the likes of the New York Times, Wired, Time, ESPN, WW Norton and Simon & Schuster.

In 2012, Anderson was commissioned by the US Postal Service (USPS) to design a commemorative stamp celebrating the 150th anniversary of the signing of the Emancipation Proclamation. She worked with USPS art director Antonio Alcala and Jim Sherraden of Nashville's Hatch Show Print to produce the final version of the stamp, which was also made into 5,000 letterpress posters. The initial run of 40,000,000 stamps sold out and the postal service released an additional edition of 10,000,000 to meet the demand.

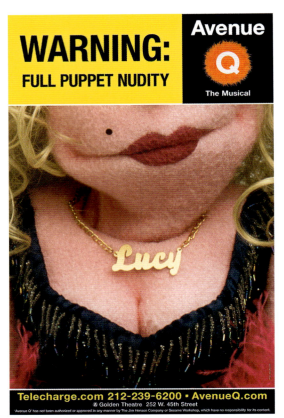

Above: A poster advertising the wildly popular Avenue Q theatre show

Her importance in design history lies not, though, just in her impressive body of work, but in the way she has consistently pushed the boundaries of what graphic design can be.

A hallmark of Anderson's design philosophy has been the importance of fun and stepping outside one's comfort zone. But she's perhaps best known for her innovative approach to typography. "Most of what I do is typography-driven, whether it's through type play or working with hierarchies in editorial content," she told Invision in 2019. "More and more, I'm interested in creating that editorial content as much as designing it—I'm all about communication through design."

Her work is included in the permanent collections of the Cooper Hewitt, Smithsonian Design Museum, the Library of Congress, and the Milton Glaser Design Archives at the School of Visual Arts.

She has won awards from the Society of Publication Designers, the Type Directors Club, The American Institute of Graphic Arts, The Art Directors Club, Graphis, and Communication Arts and Print.

"TEACHING HELPS ME STAY FRESH."

Gail Anderson

GAIL ANDERSON

In a 2022 interview with Wix Studio, she described winning the AIGA Medal in 2008, which honours lifetime achievement in graphic design, as her proudest moment. "Having my family in attendance [...] was so great," she said. "I was too nervous to enjoy the dinner or ceremony, but the evening was perfect because there was a table of Andersons in the back, complaining about how expensive it was to park in the city and looking fabulous."

Below: Another visually arresting poster for New York's School of Visual Arts

Right: Textually dramatic message from rights activist Marian Wright Edelman

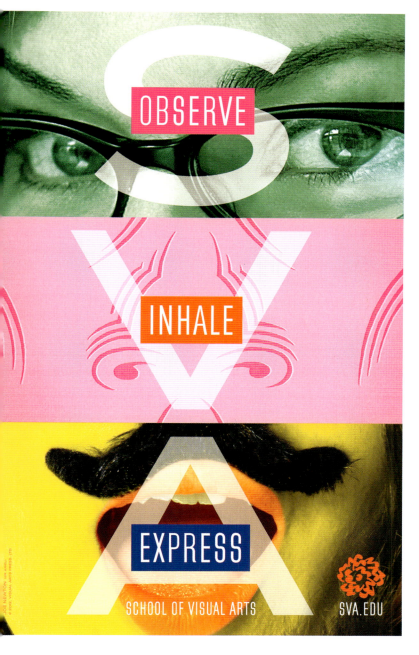

As an educator, she's played a crucial role in shaping the next generation of designers. Alongside her design work, Anderson has spent most of her career teaching at the School of Visual Arts, as well as serving on the advisory boards for Adobe Partners by Design and the Society of Publication Designers.

"I'm always surprised and a little disappointed when people say that they don't have time to 'hold the door open' for young designers," she told AIGA Eye on Design in 2018. "Not everyone wants to teach—I get it—but there are other opportunities to mentor young designers, like through internships. [...] You owe it to your profession if you had a teacher, or boss, or mentor, who helped shape your career, or even your life. It's good karma. Why risk a cartoon anvil falling on your head?"

Anderson currently serves on the board for the Type Directors Club, and is a member of the Citizens' Stamp Advisory Committee for the US Postal Service. She's also co-author with Steven Heller of 14 books on graphic design, illustration and typography.

HELLA JONGERIUS

WIDELY REGARDED AS THE WORLD'S MOST INFLUENTIAL LIVING FEMALE DESIGNER, JONGERIUS IS ADMIRED FOR HER EXCEPTIONAL EYE.

DUTCH
B. 1963

HIGHLIGHTS
Textiles, crockery, furniture

CHARACTERISTICS
Fusing old and new styles, focus on colour, irregular elements

Hella Jongerius's reputation has been built, in large part, by unifying the best of high art and mass-market design. She has also demonstrated a dogged determination to resist the demands of commercialism and prevent them from watering down her creative vision.

She was born in 1963 in De Meern, a village in the Dutch province of Utrecht. She grew up on a tomato farm, in a house that was largely devoid of culture. Her mother was a trained pattern maker and she learned knitting, pottery, and embroidery as a child. But she was uninterested in artistic pursuits because she disliked the lack of boundaries.

It was an evening course in carpentry that awakened her interest in a creative career, and in 1988 she decided to study industrial design at the Design Academy Eindhoven. Her studies were largely dominated by an adherence to Modernist thought, but she also found mentors who encouraged her to step outside these strictures, which she found incredibly liberating.

After graduating in 1993, she began work at Droog, an influential design collective started by Gijs Bakker and Renny Ramakers that launched the careers of a generation of designers including Jongerius, Richard Hutten, and Marcel Wanders. She also founded her own studio in Rotterdam called Jongeriuslab.

She quickly became known for the way her designs of a range of products—including furniture, lighting, textiles, glassware, and ceramics—fused industry and craft, high and low tech, tradition and the contemporary. One clear example of this is Red/White Vase, which is cast from the moulds of restored medieval pots. The rough casting seams, along with the potter's traditional thumbprint, give the impression of antique vessels while the strong, solid forms and use of industrial spray paint provide a contemporary look and feel.

Along similar lines, Jongerius is fascinated by the tension between the efficiency and affordability of mass production with people's desire for unique products. And she has come up with some interesting ways to square this circle. For example, her B-Set of tableware ceramics, designed in 1998 for Dutch pottery company Royal Tichelaar, is fired at an impractically high temperature during the manufacturing process. This means the clay deforms slightly, giving each object a unique shape. In a similar way Repeat Dot Print (2002), her first mass-produced fabric for textile company Maharam, featured a repeat that spans more than three metres.

One of her most celebrated designs is the Polder Sofa she designed for Vitra in 2005, which attracted

Above and below: The East River lounge chair, based on a design that was developed for the UN Lounge in collaboration with Vitra

international acclaim, despite Jongerius personally hating sofas and not having one in her home. Its blocky design, with asymmetrically placed cushions, was made to resemble the Dutch landscape, where reclaimed land is divided by dykes and canals (the word polder means a low-lying tract of land that forms an artificial hydrological entity). More broadly, Jongerius believes that sofas are often overbearing on a room, so the Polder strikes a balance between absence and presence, a strategy she applies in some way to all her designs.

Another career highlight was her work with Dutch airline KLM to transform its cabin interiors. Initially, they only asked for the textiles—seat covers, curtains, and carpets—to be redesigned. But Jongerius pushed back and persuaded them to let her redesign the seats themselves. Her designs did much to improve the passenger experience. Key elements were simplification (keeping on-board distractions to a minimum and forging unity among aesthetic elements), softening (making a homey environment through warmer, more diverse colours), and enrichment (evoking a feeling of luxury through craftsman-like details, and presenting a signature style through attention to textiles, patterns, and colours).

Other notable projects have included porcelain and earthenware design for Royal Tichelaar (1997 onwards), upholstery textile design for Maharam (2002 onwards), rugs for Danskina (2012 onwards), and the reinterpretation of classics for Finnish furniture company Artek (2013 onwards).

In 2007 Jongerius was appointed art director of colours and materials at Swiss furniture company Vitra. She told Kinfolk magazine in 2023 that she doesn't see a distinction between the two. "Colour for me is a material," she explained. "It is related to context—the object, its materiality and texture, as well as source of light and time of day. My work at Vitra has centred around creating a common library for material and colour by understanding how designers use it in a contextual way—looking at their archives, understanding their surroundings and influences."

HELLA JONGERIUS

Above: Frog table in French walnut wood, paint and epoxy

Left: Beautiful textiles for sofas and pouffes with Vitra

She has held a number of teaching positions over the years. She was a lecturer in product design at the Weißensee Kunsthochschule (Weißensee Academy of Art) Berlin from 2008–2015, head of the Living department at Design Academy Eindhoven from 2000–2004, and a teacher at Design Academy Eindhoven from 1998–1999.

In recent years Jongerius has spoken out about waste in industrial production, and has called for commercial designers to play their part by changing the system from within. In a 2015 lecture at the Design Indaba conference in Cape Town, she said, 'There's too much shopping without any social or environmental consciousness. There's too much shit design, there's too much shopping without thought. Designers have a responsibility here. I am calling for a new holistic approach to design."

That same year, she published a manifesto co-written with Dutch art and design theorist Louise Schouwenberg. "We advocate an idealistic agenda in design," it begins, "as we deplore the obsession with the New for the sake of the New, and regretfully see how the discipline lacks an intimate interweaving of the values that once inspired designers, as well as the producers of their ideas."

Since 2009 she has lived and worked in Berlin. Her work has been exhibited in numerous museums and art galleries, including London's Design Museum and Galerie Kreo in Paris.

Left: Loom Room 2022–2023, site-specific installation, loom with various textile materials

MARC NEWSON

"FUNDAMENTALLY THERE'S NO DIFFERENCE BETWEEN DESIGNING A BOAT AND DESIGNING A PEN."

Marc Newson

AUSTRALIAN
B. 1963

HIGHLIGHTS
Luxury, limited-edition designs

CHARACTERISTICS
Futuristic, fluid, refined

Opposite: A public restroom in Tokyo, Japan

Left: The Lockheed lounger

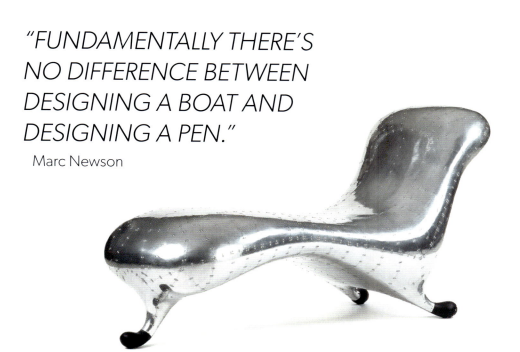

At what point does design become art, and vice-versa? That question becomes central when examining the career of Marc Newson. Perhaps more than any other living designer, he's developed a reputation for creating beautiful, exclusive, luxury, and often limited-edition products, from chairs to watches, which often become highly sought-after collector's items. But these are not "pure" art forms, because they all serve a purpose and are highly functional—often to a far more sophisticated degree than their cheaper mass-market equivalents.

Newson was born in Sydney in 1963. He developed a fascination with design from an early age after seeing the futuristic sets featured in James Bond films and Stanley Kubrick movies including *Dr. Strangelove* and *2001: A Space Odyssey*. He was introduced to architecture by his mother, who worked at Pettit+Sevitt, one of Australia's most influential and successful project home companies. His interest in product design may have stemmed from time in his grandfather's workshop fixing bicycles and repairing toys.

He studied sculpture and jewellery at Sydney College of the Arts, during which he gravitated to design furniture. He left in 1984 and, a year later, won a grant from the Australian Crafts Council that enabled him to create the first of several limited-edition chairs, including the LC1 lounge, in 1986 for a show at the Roslyn Oxley9 Gallery, then Sydney's most prestigious art space.

The LC1 was constructed by shaping aluminium panels onto a foam form hardened in fibreglass to resemble a drop of mercury; its shape has been variously described as biomorphic or zoomorphic. He later refined this design into the limited-edition Lockheed Lounge (1988–1990), which similarly played with a combination of biomorphic forms and industrial materials. It was made famous when Madonna reclined on it in the music video for her

1993 song "Rain," and has since set four world-record prices at auction for work created by a living designer.

Other early designs included the Super Guppy Lamp, an aluminium and glass industrial lamp that attaches to a vertical, curved aluminium tapered tube; the Pod of Drawers, a riveted aluminium piece inspired by the 18th-century style of 1920s French cabinetmaker André Groult; and the Embryo Chair, which is made with three legs and a chromed steel structure padded with moulded polyurethane foam.

Some of Newson's pieces were bought by Teruo Kurosaki, owner of Idée, a Japanese furniture company that represented Western designers including Philippe Starck and Marie-Christine Dorner. In 1987 Kurosaki lured Newson to Japan, where he mainly worked with Idée, and created the Charlotte Chair (1987), the three-legged carbon-fibre Black Hole Table (1988) and the Wicker Chair (1990).

During this period he began to develop a clear and identifiable style based around futuristic, alien-like forms. He finds much of his inspiration from nature, and his signature shapes are seamless, fluid, and organic. In 1991 Kurosaki organized an exhibition of Newson's latest work at the Milan Furniture Fair, and it attracted increased global attention. In the same year he moved to Paris, where he designed household products for Iittala, Alessi, and Magis; lighting for Flos; and furniture for Cappellini and Moroso. Then, in 1994, he partnered with Swiss entrepreneur Oliver Ike to found a watch company called Ikepod. Made from gold, silver, and titanium, and individually signed and numbered, the watches soon became among the most expensive and exclusive in the world.

In 1997 Newson moved to London, where he set up Marc Newson Ltd as a larger studio capable of tackling more ambitious industrial projects. One new approach was the design of vehicles, including the MN01 bicycle for Biomega (1999), the 021C concept car for Ford (1999), and the interior and livery of a privately owned jet, the Falcon 900B (1999). In 2003, he was Commissioned by the Paris art museum Fondation Cartier to design a piece of his choosing to celebrate his 40th birthday. The result was Kelvin40, a concept jet, exhibited at the museum in 2004.

In 2004, Newson partnered with Nike to design the Zvezdochka Sneaker, which was named after the

Above: The very exclusive Ikepod wristwatch, 1994

Left: MN01 bicycle for Biomega, 1999

MARC NEWSON

Above: The dashboard of the Ford 021C concept car, 1999

Russian dog that flew in Sputnik 10 in 1961, and was designed to work in a zero-G environment. Its modular design was made up of four interlocking, interchangeable parts: an outer cage, an interlocking outsole, an inner sleeve and an insole. These could be worn in multiple combinations, together or separately, for diverse functions and environments.

Significantly, these parts were fashioned from injection moulds rather than being fabricated: a revolutionary approach for the time, and one that has influenced footwear design since. As Newson told *Dezeen* in a 2014 interview, "One of the interesting things about Zvezdochka is that I approached it as a piece of industrial design. Not as a garment. […] And I think one of the big changes is that now you'll find products are much more industrially produced. It's not just a case of sewing things together any more."

Sometimes it seems that there's nothing Newson cannot design; other noteworthy creations include a 486 shotgun, a Samurai sword, and a Japanese public toilet. "My approach to design is about a set of principles that can be universally applied to anything," he told The Wall Street Journal in 2015. "The only thing that changes is material and scale. Fundamentally there's no difference between designing a boat and designing a pen."

From 2005 to 2015 he was creative director of Qantas Airways, for which he for which he completed a wide range of designs, including the luxurious first-class lounges in Melbourne and Sydney airports. In 2007 he started He started exhibiting with Gagosian Gallery, which resulted in some celebrated marble and nickel furniture designs including Extruded Tables, the Nickel Chair, and the Voronoi Shelf.

In 2013 Newson teamed up with his friend Jonathan Ive (see Chapter 46) to curate a design auction that raised $46m for The Global Fund to Fight AIDS, Tuberculosis, and Malaria. In 2014 he left Qantas and joined the team which designed the Apple Watch. In 2019 both men left Apple to found the design firm LoveFrom, which now includes the graphic designer Peter Saville.

Solo retrospectives of Newson's work have taken place around the world, and his designs are represented in many permanent collections, including the Design Museum in London, the Musée des Arts Décoratifs in Paris, and MoMA in New York.

He holds honorary doctorates from the Royal College of Art and The University of Sydney, has held adjunct professorships at The University of Sydney and Hong Kong Polytechnic University, and was appointed Royal Designer for Industry by the Royal Society of Arts. In 2012 he was awarded a CBE by Queen Elizabeth II.

Above: Extruded Table 1 extracted from a single block of marble

JONATHAN IVE

ANY LIST OF DESIGNERS THAT DID NOT INCLUDE JONATHAN IVE WOULD NOT BE WORTH ITS SALT.

BRITISH
B. 1967

HIGHLIGHTS
iMac, iPod, iPhone, iPad

CHARACTERISTICS
Minimalist aesthetic, ultra-thinness, ease of use, obsessive attention to detail

Opposite: G4 Cube, Apple

More than anyone, Jonathan Ive steered and defined the design ethos at Apple, the world's biggest and most influential product company, during his 27-year tenure. And in doing so he has had a profound influence on design and culture across the world.

Ive was born in Chingford, London in 1967, and lived there until his family moved to Stafford when he was 12. His father was a silversmith who lectured at Middlesex Polytechnic (now Middlesex University), and his grandfather was an engineer. At school he was diagnosed with dyslexia, but succeeded in getting three A grades at A-level.

According to an interview with Time magazine, it was Ive's teenage love of cars that made him decide to become a designer. However, after checking out a number of car-design courses, he shifted focus and decided to study industrial design at Newcastle Polytechnic (now Northumbria University) instead.

During his studies he was strongly influenced by the principles of the Bauhaus. His designs as a student won him an RSA Student Design Award. This enabled him to travel to Palo Alto, California, where he met design experts including Robert Brunner, who later became director of industrial design at Apple.

Ive graduated with a first-class degree in 1989. He then spent a year as an intern with his college sponsor, the product design agency Roberts Weaver Group.

Next he joined the industrials group at a London design agency called Tangerine, where he designed an array of products including microwave ovens, toilets, drills, and toothbrushes. But he became unhappy with clients who felt his designs were too costly and modern-looking.

This wasn't the case, however, when Apple became a client of Tangerine. Ive worked on what was called Project Juggernaut, investigating the future of portable computers—work that would ultimately lead to the launch of Apple's first laptop, the PowerBook, in 1991.

In 1992 Ive became a full-time employee at Apple. However, it was not until Apple co-founder Steve Jobs, who had left in 1985 following a bitter power struggle, returned in 1997 that Ive was truly able to make his mark.

This was an era when the computer was still largely seen as a business machine, and its domestic use was limited to spreadsheets, video games, and cumbersome dial-up internet connections. Ive, however, strongly believed that computers would soon become the centre of home life, and he wanted to design models that were sleek, attractive, and easy to use.

After Jobs made Ive Apple's vice-president of industrial design, his first assignment was the iMac. Introduced in 1998, it represented a leap forward in aesthetics with its translucent plastic case. It was also designed to make it easy for people to connect to the internet. An advertisement showed a seven-year-old with an iMac racing to set it up against a Stanford MBA student with a rival computer; the child left him for dust.

"ART NEEDS THE PROPER SPACE AND SUPPORT TO GROW."

Johnathan Ive

Left: The much-loved and coveted 1998 iMac

JONATHAN IVE

Left: The iPod revolutionized the way we listen to music

Up to this point, Apple's financial future had frequently seemed precarious. But the success of the iMac gave it a confidence it has never lost, and the company has recently been valued at close to $3 billion.

Ive worked on the design of many more Apple computers including the PowerBook G4, Power Mac G4 Cube, MacBook, MacBook Pro, and MacBook Air. As Jobs began to expand his vision beyond traditional computers, Ive was also instrumental in the design of three socially revolutionary devices: the iPod (2001), the iPhone (2007), and the iPad (2010).

None of these, it should be noted, were purely original inventions. Rivals had attempted digital music players, touchscreen smartphones, and computer tablets before, usually with limited success. What made the difference was Ive's minimalist vision, which emphasized visual design as much as usability and functionality, and his supreme attention to small but important design details. He was strongly influenced by Dieter Rams (see Chapter 26) and, above all, determined to keep his devices as thin as possible in an era when tech products were typically bulky, heavy, and cumbersome.

In all this, he was of one mind with Jobs. "When we were looking at objects, what our eyes physically saw and what we came to perceive were exactly the same," he told Time in 2014. "And we would ask the same questions, have the same curiosity about things."

Ive pursued his design work in ways that some saw as eccentric. For example, while researching what would become the iMac, he spent hours in a candy factory to get inspiration for the colours that would convey that this was a computer for fun as well as work. While trying to make the iPad 2 thinner than its predecessor, he flew to Japan to watch one of the nation's leading makers of samurai swords work through the night.

Ive left the company in 2019, reportedly because he'd been unhappy with the direction it had taken since Jobs's death in 2011. Explaining his decision, he stated, "Art needs the proper space and support to grow. When you're really big, that's especially important."

He founded an industrial design company called LoveFrom with fellow Apple designer Marc Newson (see Chapter 45) and graphic designer Peter Saville. In 2021 the firm announced that it was entering a partnership with Ferrari to design the carmaker's first electric vehicle. And in 2023 the firm created the official emblem for the coronation of King Charles III.

Ive was made CBE in 2006 and Knight Commander (KBE) in 2012. He is Chancellor of the Royal College of Art in London, where he effectively succeeded James Dyson (see Chapter 31) in 2017, and is involved in various charitable causes including Bono's charity Project Red.

Below: The 2007 iPhone changed the mobile market

KENNETH COBONPUE

"I WANTED THE EXPRESSION OF CREATIVITY FROM MY CHILDHOOD TO LAST FOREVER, SO I DECIDED TO MAKE IT MY LIFE'S WORK."

FILIPINO
B. 1968

HIGHLIGHTS
Furniture design, interior design

CHARACTERISTICS
Organic forms, inspiration from nature, flowing curves and lines, innovative use of materials

Left: The Phoenix car

Opposite: Rattan Yoda Chairs

Many designers talk about harnessing their love for the natural world in their creations, but often this is lip service. Kenneth Cobonpue, however, is the real deal. The multi-awarded furniture designer is a pioneer in integrating organic, natural, locally sourced materials into his constructions through traditional craft practices and modern artisanal techniques.

Cobonpue was born in 1968 in Cebu, the Philippines's second-largest city, which is known as "the Milan of Asia" because of the importance of its furniture industry. His mother, Betty, was a well-known pioneer in rattan furniture and founded her own company in 1972. This atmosphere of creativity seems to have been infectious. As a child, Cobonpue enjoyed building his own toys with the help of the craftspeople that surrounded him. In 2015 he told *Forbes* magazine, "It was an incredibly happy time, and I wanted the expression of creativity from my childhood to last forever, so I decided to make it my life's work."

Cobonpue went to study industrial design in New York in 1985. After graduating, he worked in a leather and wood workshop in Italy, then moved to Germany. After a series of further studies and apprentices abroad, Cobonpue returned to Cebu in 1996 to help manage the family business.

In 1998 he established his eponymous brand with the aim of creating an alternative to Western definitions of modern design. He developed an innovative approach based on pairing locally sourced organic materials including rattan, bamboo, abaca (a species of banana), and buri palm with handmade production techniques. In doing so, he brought together the best of nature, technology, and traditional craftsmanship to essentially reinvent modern furniture design.

Cobonpue's designs are often inspired by the lines, materials, and proportions of the islands in the Philippine archipelago. His creations are eclectic but have universal appeal. And they're carefully thought through, often with clear philosophical underpinnings.

For example, his first furniture collection in 1998, Yin & Yang, was based on the Chinese concept describing opposite but interconnected, mutually perpetuating forces. This paradox is reflected in the pieces' construction, based around alternating weaves of rattan or polyethylene strips wrapped on a rigid bent-steel frame, displaying a solid form with a transparent volume.

Later pieces took Cobonpue's love of nature in more dramatic and striking directions; 2008's Yoda Easy Chair, for example, features a mass of rattan vines, resembling tall blades of grass, forming the backrest on a steel frame. The inspiration came from the *Star Wars* character Yoda, and his famous line "We must bend, but not break."

Bends, curves, and contours are characteristic of Cobonpue's work. The self-explanatory Wave Table (2004), for example, emulates the undulation and oscillation of the ocean. Another common theme is the innovative use of natural materials. The Rapunzel Chair (2010), for instance, applies traditional braiding techniques to a thick upholstered foam tube made from a blend of acrylic and cotton, and the result is surprisingly arresting.

Cobonpue's design talents are not limited to furniture. In 2014 he won designer of the year at Maison & Objet Asia 2014 for his full-scale organic installation for Z Bar in Cebu. The unique creation featured hand-welded metals across walls and ceiling, while a cocoon-like structure made from bamboo twigs and hand-tied rattan enveloped the space and morphed into the chairs and lounge sofas.

In 2011 he designed a concept for the world's first biodegradable car, the Phoenix. Built with mostly biodegradable and recyclable materials such as bamboo, rattan, steel, and carbon fibre, it was exhibited in Milan to many raised eyebrows. It was never intended to go into production, but instead to make a point. Cobonpue pointed out that the average life of a car is five to 10 years, and the process of crushing and recycling them is costly, energy-intensive, and inefficient when compared to a biodegradable shell.

Time magazine called him "rattan's first great virtuoso," and while his designs are costly, they are much in demand. His clientele includes Hollywood stars including Angelina Jolie and Brad Pitt as well as royalty, including Queen Sofía of Spain and

Above: Yin and Yang armchair

Opposite top: Nobu restaurant in Dubai with Cobonpue's characteristic use of different materials

Left: The Wave Table, 2004

"RATTAN'S FIRST GREAT VIRTUOSO"

Time Magazine

Queen Rania of Jordan. His work has also appeared in movies including 2001's Ocean's Eleven and the TV series *CSI: Miami*.

Cobonpue has won several awards, including Hong Kong's Design for Asia Award, the Japan Good Design Award, the American Society of Interior Designers Selection, the French Coup de Coeur Award, grand prize at the Singapore International Design Competition, and Asian Designer of the Year at Maison et Objet in Paris. In September 2022 he received the first Gawad sa Sining Award for design—the highest distinction from the Cultural Center of the Philippines.

He remains modest, though, and is keen to credit the work of the company's craftsman as the real genius behind its designs. "Our dedicated craftsmen give each piece a soul as they devote their extensive time, critical minds, and expert hands to create remarkable works of art," he writes on his brand's Facebook page. "Equipped with knowledge of century-old techniques, these artisans achieve complex crafting skills through years of training in constant pursuit of mastery."

However, Cobonpue insists that he is looking not backward, but forward with his work. "Today, so many cheap things are produced by machines, and their designs reflect that," he told *WIPO Magazine* in 2012. "All over the world, there is a resurgence in craftmaking and a rekindling of the love for handmade things. At the same time, there are so many new materials and technologies that are exciting and beautiful. I would like to be at the forefront of a movement that combines innovative handmade production processes and new materials. That is the future."

Above: The Bloom armchair

ES DEVLIN

DEVLIN IS ONE OF THE WORLD'S MOST IN-DEMAND AND INFLUENTIAL SET DESIGNERS, WITH EXPERIENCE IN THEATRE, OPERA, POP CONCERTS, AND FASHION.

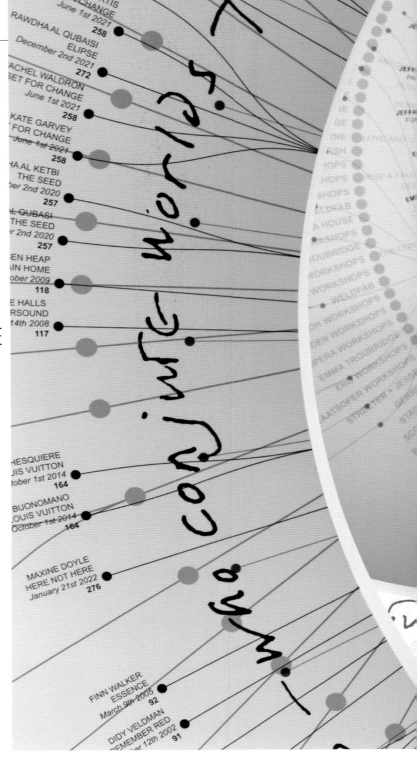

Es Devlin has collaborated with performers ranging from the Royal Ballet to Beyoncé. Arguably more than any other set designer, she has helped transform the theatre from a staid, conservative, and backward-looking medium into the colourful, innovative, and energetic world it is today.

Devlin was born in Kingston upon Thames, London, in 1971. Her mother was an English teacher and her father an education journalist for *The Times*. When she was six, the family moved to Rye, a town near the coast in East Sussex. She told *Dezeen* that this allowed her to have a "wild upbringing. We went to Beckley Woods, we picked things in the forest, we foraged."

She studied English literature at Bristol University, followed by a foundation course in fine art at Central Saint Martins in London, which she completed in 1995. She then spent a year on the Motley Theatre Design Course, which was founded at London theatre Sadler's Wells. "I found myself in this room full of people making model stuff," she said in a Netflix documentary on her career. "I thought, this is good, these people are kind of feral, and they stay up all night making models. I feel quite at home here."

Just a year later, Devlin won the Linbury Prize for Stage Design and her first commission at Bolton's Octagon Theatre. She proceeded to hone her craft at small venues including the Bush Theatre and the Gate Theatre in London before moving on to large institutions such as the National Theatre, Sadler's Wells, and the Royal Opera House.

Her work for the National Theatre began with a 1998 revival of Harold Pinter's *Betrayal*. It was set in

BRITISH
B. 1971

HIGHLIGHTS
Set design, video projections

CHARACTERISTICS
Grand scale, epic vision, attention-grabbing

Opposite: Es Devlin inside 'Iris' during 'An Atlas Of Es Devlin' exhibition, Smithson an Design Museum, New York, 2023

a hotel room in Venice, and Devlin came up with the idea of overlaying the physical sets with digital projections; this was groundbreaking at the time. Other notable stage sets include Benedict Cumberbatch's *Hamlet* at the Barbican in 2015; *Faith Healer*, in 2016, in which the Donmar Warehouse stage was framed with a chamber of synthetic rain; and *The Lehman Trilogy* in 2022, for which she won a Tony Award.

In 2003 she designed a set for post-punk band Wire's farewell gig, which saw each of the four musicians perform in their own box; that got her the attention of rapper Kanye West. She began designing regularly for concerts for West, U2, Lady Gaga, Beyoncé, The Weeknd, Jay-Z, Take That, and the Pet Shop Boys. Devlin quickly became known for creating spectacular sets that merged cutting-edge tech and video projections.

193

Left: The Poem Pavilion, Dubai, UAE

Opposite: Mirror Maze, London, UK

Devlin thinks of arenas and stadiums as saucepans, she told radio station NPR in 2023, and sees her job as to "turn up the heat and pressurize the cooker." For Beyoncé's Formation World Tour in 2016 she did just that by creating a 60 x 60 x 30-foot rotating LED box that served as a gigantic video screen. Each rotation visualized a new section of the show using image magnification (IMAG) footage, interstitials from Beyoncé's Lemonade film, and real-time VFX.

In 2017 Devlin caused a stir again with her set for singer Katy Perry's performance at the Grammy Awards. It featured a picket fence that grew into a wall—a reference to the "big, beautiful wall" President Trump was then planning to build between the US and Mexico. Devlin's work on the 2022 Super Bowl halftime show—with performers Dr. Dre, Kendrick Lamar, and Eminem—won three Emmy Awards including best production design. She has received many other awards and recognitions including a CBE, an OBE, a London Design Medal, three Olivier Awards, an Ivor Novello Award, doctorates from the Universities of Bristol and Kent and the University of the Arts London, and Royal Designer for Industry by the Royal Society for Arts.

Not only is her work highly respected, it has also had a major impact on stage and set designers. As Andrew O'Hagan wrote in *The New Yorker* in 2016, "In theatre terms, this is the age of Es Devlin. She is theatre's postmodern expert, and has an instinctive sense of how Shakespeare and opera and fashion and pop concerts might draw from the same dark web of psychological information. Each of her designs is an attack on the notion that a set is merely scenery."

Her talents have extended well beyond straight theatre and concerts. Landmark projects have included catwalk show sets for Louis Vuitton, a scent-infused mirror maze for Chanel in London, and work on the 2012 opening ceremony and 2016 closing ceremony for the Olympics. In 2020 she designed the UK Pavilion at the World Expo in Dubai. Known as the Poem Pavilion, it featured an illuminated "message to space" to which each Expo visitor would be invited to contribute. Startlingly, she was the first woman to be commissioned by the UK since world expositions began in 1851.

Below: Your Voices, Lincoln Center, New York, USA

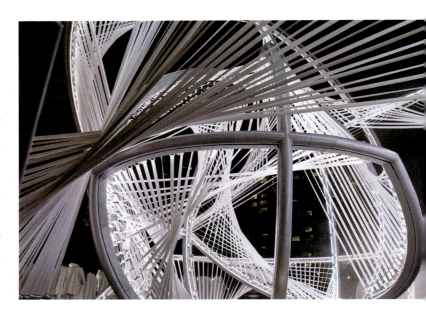

> "YOU MIGHT BE
> THE THEATRE DIRECTOR,
> YOU MIGHT BE
> THE POP STAR.
> I NEED TO JUST LISTEN."
>
> Es Devlin

But while Devlin has grand visions, they've always been created in collaboration. She is a commercial designer, not an isolated artist, and recognizes the importance of listening to clients. In 2013 she told Bloomberg how her creative process works. "I'll have my first meeting with you," she began. "You might be the theatre director, you might be the pop star. I need to just listen. I just need to understand where you're coming from. To begin with, it's kind of a diagnostic process. And then there's the first presentation, building a language.

"And then, finally, the way I describe it is kind of a dance between two imaginations. It's usually a core partnership, and each project, me and the director or me and the pop star, and our imaginations, the way I see it, dance together. And they dance with paint on their feet. And the traces left by that do become the blueprint, the map from which the design goes forward."

In an interview with *Google Arts & Culture*, Devlin said, "Once the seed happens, the next step is always drawing, and sometimes there will be looking up reference images. Usually at the end of a session of sketching and research with the studio there'll be the beginnings of an idea. Then I really do rely on my team to start to iterate, and they'll start taking the ideas further, modelling very quickly in 3D. They create various sculptural studies that relate to the sketches I've done, and then we just keep checking in with each other."

Left: Please Feed the Lions, Trafalgar Square, London, UK

CAS HOLMAN

HOLMAN DOESN'T JUST DESIGN POPULAR TOYS; SHE HAS FUNDAMENTALLY REDEFINED WHAT A TOY IS.

AMERICAN
B. 1974

HIGHLIGHTS
Rigamajig, Geemo

CHARACTERISTICS
Designing toys, objects, and spaces that encourage learning through play

Right: Rigamajig Basic Builder Kit

Opposite: Space design by Holman for 14th Street Y Movescape, New York, USA

The crux of Cas Holman's philosophy is that rather than a toy being prescriptive—it has to be played with in a certain way—it should be open-ended, allowing the child to decide how to interact with it. In this way she encourages creativity in children through unstructured play.

The inspiration for this approach can be seen in her childhood. She was born in Oceanside, California, and describes herself as a "latchkey kid" who spent summers exploring the wilderness. When the family moved to Morgan Hill in Santa Clara, California, her mother worked at a Montessori school, which places an emphasis on hands-on learning and developing real-world skills. These principles resonated with her and influenced the way she raised her own kids.

Her stepfather, Tim, was a mechanic and his playful nature was a big influence on her. "We struggled financially, but still had fun," Holman recalls. "We made our own way, for sure. The way my family functioned looked nothing like any of my peers' families. I noticed, but it didn't bother me much. Tim left when I was around 12 and my mom didn't remarry. My mom, my sister and I were all pretty independent."

After attending Montessori preschool and kindergarten, Holman and her family moved to Grass Valley in Nevada County, California. She spent a great deal of time in the ceramics studio, and adored her horticulture teacher. Later, she took a BFA in Feminist Theory with a minor in Fine Art at the University of California, Santa Cruz. Partway through her studies, she took an extended break to work for her aunt and uncle at a research station in the Galapagos Islands.

She graduated in June 1998 and took an MFA in 3D Design at Cranbrook Academy of Art in Bloomfield Hills, Michigan. It was there that she became interested in toys and in designing for children.

"It was 2003, and my work was getting more interactive and playful," she recalls. "My work has always been humorous, but I was finding myself making things more explicitly playful to interact with. More movement, unpredictability, silliness."

After completing her MFA in 2005, Holman launched Heroes Will Rise, an independent toy company with a Brooklyn workshop focusing on learning tools and spaces designed in the spirit of invention and creativity. The ethos of these products is idealistic, optimistic, and rooted in the belief that imagination is an essential part of childhood. They are never gender-specific, and encourage an exploratory, unstructured play.

"Most toys come with pre-defined identities and stories, which rob children of the joy of imagining these things," she told *Fast Company* in 2015. "There is also a dearth of open-ended toys, or toys without instructions and right and wrong answers. This leaves few opportunities to figure out how to use a toy, experiment, fail, and invent the story of where it came from, and why it does what it does. Imagining, understanding, and becoming who we are is a process informed by play, and both toy companies and designers are taking all the exploration out of it."

Her first product, Geemo, was a flexible toy with magnetic limbs that attract and repel each other in unpredictable ways. It was inspired by patterns in nature and the idea of units that form irregular patterns and join together into larger units. The magnetic limbs were left unmarked and uncoloured; Holman felt there was something wonderful about kids not knowing whether any two limbs would attract or repel until they tried it.

Above: Rigamajig Basic Builder components for making a cart

Below: Rigamajig Basic Builder kit with chutes add-on

Holman was also involved in the development of Imagination Playground blocks. The large yet lightweight foam building blocks allow children to build their own pop-up playgrounds. The system was developed in partnership with early childhood specialists and the NYC Parks Department, and can be found in schools, children's museums, and playgrounds around the world.

Similar principles of empowering kids through play led her to launch Rigamajig in 2006. The line of collaborative "construction debris," as Holman has referred to it, was originally developed as the Children's Workyard Kit, a custom play feature for the High Line in New York. Featuring elements such as wooden play pieces, ropes and pulleys, nuts and bolts, Rigamajig playsets give children broad scope to combine different elements and make unique constructions.

"THERE'S A NUANCE BETWEEN PRETEND AND IMAGINATION"

Cas Holman

The individual pieces are large and require multiple hands to connect them, encouraging kids to learn collaboration and communication skills as well as unlocking their imagination. In this light, such toys stand in stark contrast to those that dictate how they should be played with.

Holman has shared her design ideas and skills with others through teaching. From 2009 to 2012 she was an assistant professor at Syracuse University, then taught from 2012 to 2022 as an associate professor at the Rhode Island School of Design.

Her ideas are not wholly original; she's building on the concepts and philosophies of academics and toy designers who went before her. But what's important is how she's put these ideas into practice so successfully.

Below: Playground and exhibition at the Liberty Science Center, New Jersey, USA

Her work has also dovetailed productively with similar movements, such as AnjiPlay, an educational philosophy and approach created in China by Cheng Xueqin, with whom Holman has collaborated.

In 2019 Holman was the subject of an episode of the Netflix series *Abstract: The Art of Design* titled "Cas Holman: Design for Play." In the documentary, she discusses the core of her philosophy of toy making. "There's a nuance between pretend and imagination," she says. "If we always give children toys that have this story built into it, we rob them of the opportunity to invent the story and make up the story themselves. The moments that I see things I wouldn't have thought of, that's when I know it's been successful… when it has a life of its own that kids are inventing things I couldn't have, I didn't think of. I didn't design it to do that, but they made it do that."

THAI/AMERICAN
B. 1974

HIGHLIGHTS
Creative direction, design leadership

CHARACTERISTICS
Storytelling approach, playful experimentation, global influences

Below: Harper Macaw Political Collection

PUM LEFEBURE

"…GOOD DESIGN HAS THAT POWER TO STICK WITH YOU AND HAS LASTING IMPACT"

Pum Lefebure was born and raised in Bangkok, Thailand to academic parents who had met in medical school. She recalls being a shy child who was obsessed with all things visual, including the colourful fabrics her mother would take her shopping for, and the beautiful temples she'd pass by during bus journeys to school.

Left and below: Rebrand for a new paper line for Neenah

Her mother enrolled her in art lessons every Saturday, where she developed her skills in drawing and painting with watercolours and oils. Her favourite "toy" growing up was a set of 36 coloured pencils, which she'd use for hours to create her own imaginary worlds. By the time she was attending a conservative Catholic school, her collection had grown to over 200 pencils, which she meticulously arranged by hues and shades.

A pivotal moment came when she first saw the United Colors of Benetton 1991 ad by Oliviero Toscani that showed a priest and a nun kissing. "When I saw that [...] I knew I wanted to have a career in design and advertising," she later told Muse by Clios. "The ad was so powerful and provocative—it made you think and rethink, yet remember the brand."

At the age of 18, during her senior year of high school, Lefebure arrived in the United States as an exchange student. She excelled in art classes there, and worked tirelessly to improve her English and maintain good grades in all subjects. This dedication paid off when she earned a partial scholarship to Radford University in Virginia, where she secured a summa cum laude BFA in Graphic Design.

After graduation, she began an internship at Supon Design Group in Washington D.C. Her innovative approach to job applications—sending out a handmade, velvet resume—highlighted her willingness to think outside the box, and stand out from the crowd. It got her hired on the spot.

During her nearly eight years at the agency, Lefebure worked her way up from intern to designer, senior designer, art director and finally senior art director. Her work ethic did not go unnoticed: she was often the first to arrive and the last to leave the office. This dedication was partly driven by her status as a non-U.S. citizen, which added pressure to perform exceptionally to maintain her work visa.

In 2003, she co-founded Design Army in Washington D.C with her husband Jake, whom she'd met at work. "We basically worked all the time and we figured that since we got along great there, it could only get better if we were 100 percent committed," she later told *Creative Boom* magazine.

The couple started the company out of their home, and moved into an office the following year. This move marked the beginning of Lefebure's journey as not just a designer, but as an entrepreneur and business leader. Under her leadership, the agency has developed numerous international campaigns for high-profile clients such as Adobe, Morphe, Neenah, Netflix, PepsiCo, Smithsonian Institution, The Ritz-Carlton and the White House Historical Association.

One of their most celebrated projects, however, was done pro-bono. One night, she offered their services to the Washington Ballet after meeting the artistic director at a party. Design Army went on to craft every aspect of a commemorative book titled *Wonderland* which was used to raise awareness and donations for the ballet's youth programs.

They've worked with the company on many projects since, including performances of Sleepy Hollow, Ernest Hemingway's The Sun Also Rises and Alice in Wonderland. Other notable projects include the music video for electro-pop group Shaed's hit single Trampoline; a sumptuous and highly-styled campaign for Georgetown Optician, 'Eyes Say More Than Words'; a limited edition line of chocolate bars for bean-to-bar conservationists Harper Macaw; and an integrated campaign for CityCenterDC, a landmark mixed-use development.

On all these projects and more, one of the things that's set Lefebure apart has been her ability to bring a global sensibility to American design.

Above: The Washington Ballet *Wonderland* book

Left: A campaign for Georgetown opticians

Opposite: A poster for HK Ballet, 2018

"I THINK GOOD DESIGN IS SOMETHING THAT PLEASES THE EYES AND ACTIVATES THE MIND."

Pum Lefebure

Her creative point of view draws from different cultures and resonates with diverse audiences, making her work truly international in scope.

This unique perspective is most evident in partnerships such as the Hong Kong Ballet 40th Anniversary campaign, which she's called one of her proudest achievements. Taking Ravel's Boléro and integrating subtle layers of sound design that nod to the pop culture cue of classic Kung Fu films, Design Army told a series of stories through music. In doing so, they helped rebrand what's often seen as a traditional and inaccessible art form into a joyful and relatable experience.

"I think it's quite simple for me: I think good design is something that pleases the eyes and activates the mind," she told *Veritrope* in 2015. "You see a lot of good design that's really pretty or beautiful… but I just don't think that's enough. [...] Does that particular design give you goosebumps? Is your spinal cord tingling? It's that physical response that you can't really explain what it is, but you know, good design has that power to stick with you and has lasting impact."

Lefebure has earned a plethora of awards, from organizations such as Cannes Lions, Emmy Awards, D&AD, One Show, ADC, AIGA365, SPD, and TDC. She now regularly judges global design contests herself, and has served as jury President for Cannes Design Lions, One Show Design, The Clios and London International Awards. She has also lectured and led workshops around the world, and currently serves as Vice Chairman on the Board of Directors for The One Club in New York.

NAIHAN
LI

NAIHAN LI IS ONE OF THE MOST PROMINENT FIGURES IN CHINESE DESIGN.

CHINESE
B. 1981

HIGHLIGHTS
Crates series,
I Am a Monument series

CHARACTERISTICS
Experimental, unconventional, fusion of tradition and modernity

Above: The Crates Bar Design

Opposite: The Crates Wardrobe design

With a background in architecture, Naihan Li has been hugely influential on her contemporaries thanks to her success in incorporating traditional Chinese crafts into the making of contemporary design works.

She was born in 1981 in Harbin, in Heilongjiang, China's northernmost province, and moved to Beijing as a child in the mid-1980s. She studied at the Bartlett School of Architecture in London before returning to Beijing, where she first collaborated with artist Ai Weiwei. On that project she served as a coordinator for the Jinhua Architecture Park in eastern China, which contains 17 specially designed pavilions by Chinese and international architects.

Li went on to work as an independent architect and designer for a range of projects. One of her first constructions was Keruo Space, an area for creative businesses in Caochangdi, an arts district in northeast Beijing. Another was Royal Kitchen, a restaurant and shop inside the Forbidden City, the historical imperial palace complex at the heart of Beijing.

Below: I Am a Monument, CCTV Wardrobe

In 2006 Li co-founded BAO Atelier Hong Kong, a company that specialized in art exhibition and book design. It was a good time to be starting a creative business; that year, the general secretary of the Chinese Communist Party, Hu Jintao, declared that he wanted to see the country move from "made in China" to "designed in China." This led to a wave of new design companies, museums, events, and educational institutions. As a result, today China has more design students than any other nation.

Early projects for BAO Atelier included *Aftershock: Contemporary British Art for the British Council*; it was the first exhibition of its kind in that it was created for a Chinese audience. BAO Atelier also produced a China Business Guide for Santander Bank and performed creative research for Nike relating to the 2008 Beijing Olympics.

In 2009 Li was a featured artist and exhibition designer for the e-arts festival New Media Archaeology in Shanghai and the exhibition *Emporium* in Milan. The following year she launched her own furniture design studio, and has since created and produced all her works in-house.

Above: The Birmingham Library Side Table

The laboratory nature of Li's workshop is the foundation of her exploration into material and form. She specializes in combining cutting-edge design tools and production technology with the fine craftsmanship available in China. She sees her studio as a playground where her personal experiences and droll sense of humour guide the making process, with the aim of creating contemporary Chinese design.

In 2011 Li came to world attention with her most famous creation to date. Exhibited as part of Beijing Design Week, The Crates were mobile furniture objects, made of black walnut or industrial-style stainless steel with a mirrored finish, that conceal their true functions until unlocked or unfolded. They appear to be shipping crates, but they become modular items of everyday furniture such as bookshelves, beds, and armchairs.

NAIHAN LI

Above: A chair in the metal Crates series

These objects were inspired by the transience Li saw in Beijing, where migrant workers flock in their millions each year. The Crates reimagine furniture as not simply functional, but modular and mobile. It can also be seen as a statement on fringe neighbourhoods, where artists congregate, which are regularly scheduled for demolition. The product was nominated for 2012 Design of the Year by London's Design Museum.

Another project that drew international interest was the I Am a Monument series, which turns well-known buildings such as the New York Stock Exchange, the Pentagon, and the United Nations headquarters into items of furniture. The Pentagon, for instance, becomes a bed.

The most famous piece in the series is the CCTV Wardrobe, an angular, dramatically cantilevered piece of furniture made in 2014, which is based on the unusually shaped China Central Television building in Beijing, designed by Dutch architectural practice OMA. The wardrobe has been officially acquired by the M+ museum in Hong Kong, and was featured in its design department's inaugural exhibition.

I Am a Monument is the most obvious example of how Li fuses her architectural background with her furniture design skills. Other noteworthy projects include her collaboration with department-store chain Lane Crawford, with her metal crate Hydroponic Garden Wardrobe collection (2014); her design of Yuz Museum Shanghai's café (2015); Superbenches, a development project aimed at revitalizing the Stockholm suburb of Järfälla (2017); a virtual-reality installation at the Shanghai Himalayas Museum, a response to Leonardo da Vinci's deluge sketches (2017); and production design for Jiang Wen's Chinese action-comedy film *Hidden Man* (2018).

Li has been commissioned by a range of global institutions and brands including the Goethe Institute, Lane Crawford, and Swarovski. Her limited-edition design works are held by private collectors around the world and have been exhibited at museums including M+, London's Design Museum, Yuz Museum Shanghai, and Sifang Art Museum in Nanjing; and at international events including the Milan Triennial, the Venice Biennial, Design Miami, and the Gwangju Design Biennial.

Above: 100% All Natural, a furniture series that explores aesthetics in an eccentric way with the use of the traditional craft of lacquer

PICTURE CREDITS

ALAMY
10: The National Trust Photolibrary
11: Lebrecht Music & Arts
16: Arcaid Images
18: Charles Hosea / VIEW
19: The Dragons chair: Marco Secchi Eileen Gray exhibition: Stanley Baxter
20–21: Shawshots
22: Underwood Archives, Inc
23: 1958 Cadillac eldorado Brougham: CNP Collection
24: Bo Arrhed
25: Maidun Collection
26: Niels Poulsen
27: Paul Sorensen
32: Heritage Image Partnership Ltd
34: Bosiljka Zutich
35: Keith Van-Loen
46: Heritage Image Partnership Ltd
47: Top image: Kommersant Photo Agency
47: Bottom image: Andreas von Einsiedel
48: YA/BOT
49: dpa picture alliance
49: Portrait of Eva Zeisel: Peter Tobia/ Philadelphia Inquirer / Sipa US
50: Peter Tobia/Philadelphia Inquirer / Sipa US
52: Elizabeth Whiting & Associates
57: Chronicle
58: Maurice Savage
59: Whitworth Art Gallery
61: Randy Duchaine
62: Lordprice Collection
63: Top image: Neil Baylis
64: Grant Smith / VIEW
66 & 67: Grant Smith / VIEW
72: JJs
73: Top image: Everett Collection Inc
73: Bill Waterson
74: Top image: ruelleruelle
74: Bottom image: TCD/Prod.DB
75: Both images: Everett Collection Inc
79: AP Photo/Charles Dharapak
79: Bottom image: adsR
93: AP Photo/Kyodo News
96: YA/BOT
98 Richard Levine
98–99: Both images: Randy Duchaine
100: Hemis
101: Goddard Archive Portraits
103: Top image: Carolyn Jenkins
103: WENN Rights Ltd
104–105: INTERFOTO
104: Goddard Archive Portraits
105: BTEU/TEKNISKA
106: Top image: INTERFOTO
106: Bottom image: cm studio
107: Chris Mattison
109: Neil Spence
110: Top image: Simon Webster
116: Sandro Michahelles/Sintesi
116–117: Jeff Gilbert
118–119: John Gaffen
118: Chris Brennan
120: ROUX Olivier/SAGAPHOTO.COM
121: Retro AdArchives

134: AP Photo/Atlanta Journal-Constitution, Jessica McGowan
135: Chris Willson
137: Portrait of Philippe Starck: Hemis
150 Top image: B Christopher
150: Bottom image: Sandy Young
156: Portrait of Naoto Fukusawa: Danny Nebraska
156–157: KEYSTONE/Georgios Kefalas
158: lm_photography
159: Yoshio Tsunoda/AFLO/Alamy Live News
185: Steve Speller
186: trekandshoot
195: Top image: ukartpics

GAIL ANDERSON
172–175: all images courtesy Gail Anderson
SVA "Make it Here" Poster
Designers: Gail Anderson and Joe Newton, Martin Beck Theater "Man of La Mancha" Poster
Designer: Gail Anderson, SpotCo
Illustrators: Ward Schumaker and James Victore, Golden Theater "Avenue Q" Poster
Designer: Gail Anderson; SpotCo,
SVA "Observe, Inhale, Express" Poster
Designers: Gail Anderson and Joe Newton, Chicago Design Museum Marian Wright Edelman Poster Designer: Gail Anderson

BRIDGEMAN ART LIBRARY
56, 42: Portrait of Princess Elizabeth wearing Groag's Tulip print dress: Granger
44: Christie's image
45: Picture Alliance/DPA
51: Indianapolis Museum of Art / Gift of Dr. Steven Conant
53: Christie's Images
63: Bottom image: Granger

KENNETH COBONPUE
188–191: all images courtesy of Kenneth Cobonpue

CREATIVE COMMONS
9, 17

DANIEL LEWANDOWSKI
60: www.paulrand.design

ROBIN AND LUCIENNE DAY
68–71

DESIGN ARMY
201: Portrait of Pum Lefebure: Jacopo Moschin
200–203: all images courtesy Design Army

GARLAND
31: Permission to use image of Harry Beck courtesy of Wanda Garland

GETTY IMAGES
53: Photo mural of Ray and Charles Eames: Ken Lubas/ Los Angeles Times
65: Ray Fisher
76: John Kisch Archive

97: Gabriela Herman
132–133: Thomas S England
192-3: Cindy Ord

HELSINKI DESIGN MUSEUM
84: Portrait of Maija Isola

HENK W. GIANOTTEN
90–91: Portrait of Adrian Frutiger

HELLA JONGERIUS
176–177: Marc Eggimann
177: Marcus Gaab for Vitra
179: Frog Table: Fabrice Gousset, courtesy Galerie kreo
176–179: all other images courtesy Hella Jongerius

CAS HOLMAN
196: Portrait of Cas Holman: Thalassa Raasch
196–199: all images courtesy of Cas Holman

NAIHAN LI
204–207: all images courtesy of Naihan Li

KARE.COM
148: Portrait of Susan Kare
151: Picture of Susan Kare at work

KEVIN KEANE
81: Portrait of Jacqueline Casey from the collection of Kevin Keane

LONDON TRANSPORT MUSEUM
28-29, 30: TfL from the London Transport Museum collection

MARIMEKKO
84-87: Maija Isola patterns

MARC NEWSON
180–183: all images courtesy of Marc Newson
181: Prudence Cuming Associates, courtesy Gagosian

PAOLA NAVONE
140: Crate & Barrel
141: Portrait of Paola Navone: Enrico Conti
141: Top image: Crate & Barrel
141: Bottom image: Gervasoni
142–143: Crate & Barrel
143: Serax

PENTAGRAM NEW YORK
128–131

KARIM RASHID
164–165, 167: all images courtesy of Karim Rashid
166: Amy Hunter Photography

ROCHESTER INSTITUTE OF TECHNOLOGY
80–83: Jacqueline Casey posters, RIT Cary Graphic Arts Collection

SAGMEISTER INC

168–171: All images courtesy of Sagmeister Inc

ART SIMS
152–155: all images courtesy Art Sims

ERIK SPIEKERMANN
124–127: images courtesy of Erik Spiekermann

SHUTTERSTOCK
8, 10–11, 13, 32-33, 54, 55, 108
5: Dyson vacuum umitc, Eames chair/ Shutterstock-Pixelsquid
6: Alex Segre
7: Karolis Kavolelis
12: Evgeniyqw
14: Monster_Design
15: Gaschwald
23: 1960 Chevrolet Corvette: Meunierd
54: Top image: Khemsingh Kawarkshatri
55: Eames House: Stephanie Braconnier
67: Bottom image: Shutterstock/Pixelsquid
77: Steve Cukrov
78: Top image: Jeff Whyte
78: Bottom image: Chie Inoue
92: Pond Thananat
93: Top image: pixible
94: Nithid Memanee
95: Philip Pilosian
102: Alex Segre
110: Bottom image: Ron Ellis
111: Art-Dolgov
119: Ned Snowman
122: umitc
123: Top image: umitc
123: Bottom image: Anna Hoychuk
149: tomeqs
184: Karolis Kavolelis
187: Both images: marleyPug
194: Abie Davies
194: Right image: lev radin
195: Bottom image: Martin Helgemeir

STARCKNETWORK
138: Top image, 139
136: gdelaubier
137 & 138: Starcknetwork/Kartell

ROSMARIE TISSI
112–115: images courtesy of Rosmarie Tissi

UNIVERSITY OF BRIGHTON DESIGN ARCHIVES
41: 1959 Portrait of Jacqueline Groag: John Garner

UNIVERSITY COLLEGE CORK, IRELAND
36–39: Special Collections & Archives, UCC Library

UNIVERSITY OF FASHION & PALM SPRINGS ART MUSEUM
40–43: Francesca Sterlacci

CHRISTOPHER GARCIA VALLE
128: Portrait of Paula Scher

ACKNOWLEDGEMENTS

I'd like to thank Vanessa Daubney and the team at Arcturus, whose invaluable guidance helped me raise my writing game and craft a text of which I could be truly proud.

I'm also indebted to Lisa Hillman, whose eagle-eyed editing picked up ambiguities and inconsistencies in my work that I'd never have spotted myself.

Finally, and most importantly, I thank my beloved Julie, who's been my biggest cheerleader, from patiently reading drafts to offering invaluable feedback. She means everything to me.